MW00677358

Shakespeare's Perfume

Shakespeare's Perfume

Sodomy and Sublimity in the Sonnets, Wilde, Freud, and Lacan

RICHARD HALPERN

PENN

UNIVERSITY OF PENNSYLVANIA PRESS

Philadelphia

10 9 8 7 6 5 4 3 2 1

Published by
University of Pennsylvania Press
Philadelphia, Pennsylvania 19104-4011

Library of Congress Cataloging-in-Publication Data

Halpern, Richard, 1954–
    Shakespeare's perfume : sodomy and sublimity in the Sonnets, Wilde, Freud, and Lacan /
Richard Halpern.
        p. cm.
    Includes bibliographical references (p.) and index.
    ISBN 0-8122-3661-0 (acid-free paper)
    1. Shakespeare, William, 1564–1616. Sonnets. 2. Shakespeare, William, 1564–1616—In
literature. 3. Wilde, Oscar, 1854–1900. Portrait of Mr W.H. 4. Freud, Sigmund, 1856–1939.
Kindheitserinnerung des Leonardo da Vinci. 5. Lacan, Jacques, 1901– Ethique de la
psychanalyse, 1959–1960. 6. Sonnets, English—History and criticism—Theory, etc.
7. Psychoanalysis and literature. 8. Sublime, The, in literature. 9. Sodomy in literature.
I. Title.
PR2848 .H25 2002
820.9'353—dc21   2002018063

Contents

Introduction

Sodomy and the sublime: once the pleasures of alliteration have faded, it is not at all clear what might connect the two. Sodomy is primarily a legal and theological category whose heyday was the medieval and early modern periods. The sublime is an aesthetic category that originated with Longinus but flourished in the eighteenth and nineteenth centuries. So the two terms inhabit not only different and apparently unrelated discourses but also distant historical and cultural moments. The temporal problem is perhaps the less serious of the two, since the category of the sublime often seems to be applied after the fact. Longinus detects it in Homer, who surely lacked any inkling of the concept; Edmund Burke finds it in Milton, who at least had read Longinus, as well as in Shakespeare and Spenser, who had not. So if the conjoining of sodomy and sublimity seems anachronistic, at least anachronism is built into one of the two terms. Still, other problems remain. Sodomy has generally denoted a class of nonprocreative sexual activities (usually but not always same-sex activities) for which one might be denounced, prosecuted, or executed. Sublimity is a class of aesthetic phenomena associated variously with grandeur, exaltation, the experience of fear or pain, and the limits of representation. Both categories have been so diversely construed that they are fuzzy around the edges, but it isn't intuitively obvious how they might overlap, either logically or culturally. Sodomy doesn't engross much space in treatises on aesthetics, and aesthetic issues, conversely, don't much preoccupy the jurists and theologians who define sodomitical acts.

Things seem less dire if we shift categories a bit and speak of sexuality and aesthetics, for here we find a rich tradition, from Plato to Freud, connecting erotic (often homoerotic) desire and artistic creation or transcendent experience. Freud's concept of sublimation, in which sexual drives are diverted to nonsexual (often artistic) aims, will provide a kind of guiding thread for much of this study, although I take it as a culminating point of the tradition I wish to explore rather than a theoretical postulate, and I will also examine certain themes that run distinctly against the Freudian grain. The very word sublimation suggests a connection with the sublime which I will develop in every chapter of this book, not only those on Freud and Lacan. Sublimation as a psychoanalytic concept draws on older alchemical traditions of purification, separation, and (surprisingly) defeminization, which will also come into play.

I turn to Oscar Wilde, however, to provide a first set of connections as well as tensions between the sexual and aesthetic spheres. Wilde's novella *The Portrait of Mr. W.H.* depicts the catastrophic results of a theory about Shakespeare's sonnets that circulates in hothouse fashion among a coterie of young men. There is much swooning over the beauty of the sonnets and of the young man they depict, all of which serves to displace the desire that Wilde's characters feel for one another. Lawrence Danson wryly notes that "for many of Wilde's readers, both before and after the trials, this 'rationalization of homosexual desire as aesthetic experience' (in Elaine Showalter's phrase) was a verbal fig-leaf bulging with phallic reality."[1] Such a response was not wrongheaded; indeed, it was probably just what Wilde demanded of his readers. One might even argue that part of Wilde's project in the *Portrait* is to push the "fig-leaf" model to the point of breakdown. At the same time, however, this strategy reveals certain difficulties with the model itself insofar as it reduces the aesthetic to a mere surface phenomenon covering the truth of forbidden sexual desire. For one thing, aesthetic experience could not substitute for sexuality at all if it did not already offer a sensual intensity that rivals (or at least evokes) that of its counterpart. Second, it is not at all clear that (homo)sexuality is the hidden "truth" of aesthetic experience for Wilde; it seems more accurate to say that for him aesthetic experience is both the "truth" and the origin of sexual desire. This, I will argue, is an idea that Wilde borrows from Shakespeare, and it turns Freudian sublimation on its head. It is to be found as well in a passage from St. Paul to which I shall soon turn. The aesthetic origins of sexuality is a recurrent motif in the tradition I trace in this book.

But even if we accept the idea that aesthetic experience provided Wilde with a kind of fig-leaf for the love that dare not speak its name, his discursive situation has now been precisely reversed. On the one hand, openly addressing homoerotic themes when discussing Shakespeare's Sonnets is now perfectly acceptable, indeed unavoidable—unless, that is, one happens to be Helen Vendler. I myself frequently enjoy the pleasurable *frisson* of springing sonnet 20 and its "master mistress" on unsuspecting groups of undergraduates. On the other hand, I would be rendered squirmingly uncomfortable were I told to teach a class on the *beauty* of Shakespeare's sonnets. And I believe that I'm not alone in this. Thus if what was unspeakable for Wilde (let's call it sodomy) is now perfectly speakable for us, yet what was once speakable for Wilde (let's call it beauty) has now become somehow unspeakable—or at least less speakable—for us. This reversal of positions is the product of a complex history, but its possibility depends, I believe, partly on the fact that sodomy, from the very inception of the concept, is implicated in certain aesthetic categories, in particular that category known as the sublime.

The chronological starting point for this connection is a passage in St. Paul's Epistle to the Romans. I address this passage in my first chapter and don't want to anticipate too much of that argument here. Briefly, however: the passage claims that the Greeks were afflicted with homosexuality as divine punishment for worshiping statues. This is an odd moment in an odd but brilliant writer. Paul's particular way of articulating same-sex acts and idolatry posits the former not only as the enemy of the unrepresentable God but also, more strangely, as his counterpart, a situation that continues in later descriptions of sodomy as the unspeakable vice. Sodomy is thus placed in that "beyond" of representation known as the sublime. More specifically, it is brought into proximity with a Hebraic sublime, associated with the Mosaic ban on images. Hebrew scripture has been associated with the sublime ever since Longinus and is cited in the writings of eighteenth-century writers on the sublime such as Burke and Kant. But it was Hegel who, in his *Aesthetics*, ties the concept of the sublime most intimately and powerfully to Hebrew scripture. I shall discuss Hegelian sublimity in my chapter on Freud, but I should also say that it influences this entire book, though sometimes only implicitly.

My thesis is that Paul's equation of sodomy and sublimity in Romans is elaborated by medieval theologians and given aesthetic form by Shakespeare's Sonnets. The Sonnets, in turn, powerfully influence Oscar Wilde's later "invention" of homosexuality as both an identity and an aesthetic. The emergence of modern homosexuality does not cancel the older ties between sodomy and sublimity, however, but simply reworks them in new guises. Freud's little book on Leonardo da Vinci and Jacques Lacan's writings on sublimation in his Seventh Seminar exemplify this. I would claim, then, that the four works examined in this book are not randomly chosen but form part of a coherent tradition, a tradition I could easily have extended both laterally and forward to such contemporary writers as William Burroughs. I have limited myself to a few outstanding instances, however, on the theory that less is more.

Earlier I made the somewhat tongue in cheek remark that writers of treatises on aesthetics do not spend much time discussing sodomy. This is not to say that the issue of homoeroticism does not ever put in an appearance. Here I shall note two moments in which homosexual desire inflects the concept of beauty in philosophical aesthetics, as a kind of general prologue to my more specific investigation of sodomy and the sublime. The first example comes from Edmund Burke's *A Philosophical Enquiry into the Origin of Our Ideas of the Sublime and the Beautiful* (1757). At the beginning of the Third Part of the *Enquiry*, Burke first turns to the concept of beauty, which he defines as "that quality or those qualities in bodies by which they cause love, or some passion similar to it" (83).[2] He adds that he "confine[s] this definition to the merely sensible qualities of things" (83), meaning that he speaks of a love that attaches not to the personalities or the spiritual qualities of loved persons but only to their visible attributes as bodies. It might seem, then, that when Burke speaks of "love" he means "desire," but he insists that this is not so:

> I likewise distinguish love, by which I mean that satisfaction which arises to the mind upon contemplating anything beautiful, of whatsoever nature it may be, from desire or lust; which is an energy of the mind, that hurries us on to the possession of certain objects, that do not affect us as they are beautiful, but by means altogether different. We shall have a strong desire for a woman of no remarkable beauty; whilst the greatest beauty in men, or in other animals, though it causes love, yet excites nothing at all of desire. (83)

Having first defined the beautiful as that which causes love, Burke then defines love, tautologically, as the mind's reaction to beauty. The two examples by which he proceeds to distinguish love from desire are parallel but asymmetrical to the logic of his argument. The "woman of no remarkable beauty" arouses desire but not love. She therefore falls outside the sphere of Burke's investigation entirely. Although she plays the functional role of distinguishing an aesthetic passion or sensation from a non-aesthetic one, she is not herself a proper object for aesthetic contemplation. By contrast, the man (or animal) who causes love but not desire does constitute a legitimate object for aesthetic reflection—doubly legitimate, in that he provokes the proper impulse and does not arouse the improper one. The very possibility of the beautiful as something that excites a passion distinct from desire therefore depends on the non-existence of male homoerotic desire. This is not just a case of any absence, but of a determinate absence that nevertheless provides a structural support. Burke could easily have found exemplary objects—a vase, a flower—in which the question of sexual desire would not have arisen at all. But he seems compelled to bring the question of beauty into dangerous propinquity with lust so as then to purge it as best he can.

Purgation, as we shall see in my chapter on Shakespeare's Sonnets, plays an important role in the aesthetic tradition that this book explores. Burke's contrast between the beautiful man and the "woman of no remarkable beauty" recalls, in fact, the Sonnets' pairing of the beautiful young man and the so-called Dark Lady, whose "face hath not the pow'r to make love groan" (131: 6) but who nevertheless exerts an inexplicable sexual attraction on Shakespeare and, moreover, draws to herself all the sodomitical attributes that are carefully expunged from the young man. Burke does not mention sodomy directly in the opening passages on beauty, but by linking (non-)desire for men with that for animals, he obliquely evokes the fact that English law had for centuries united homosexuality and bestiality under the category of "buggery." (A statute passed in 1533, for instance, outlawed "the detestable and abhomynable vice of buggery committed with mankynde or beaste.")[3] Burke therefore knew, and indirectly tells us he knew, that same-sex desire was possible, since the very existence of buggery laws attests to it. But such desire will be definitionally excluded from the field of the aesthetic.

Having made, as best he can, the requisite distinctions to define beauty, Burke sums up:

Which shews that beauty, and the passion caused by beauty, which I call love, is different from desire, though desire may sometimes operate along with it; but it is to this latter that we must attribute those violent and

> tempestuous passions, and the consequent emotions of the body which
> attend what is called love in some of its ordinary acceptations, and not to
> the effects of beauty merely as such. (83)

In provoking "violent and tempestuous passions," desire spawns a turbu-
lence more akin to the sublime than to the beautiful. Male homoerotic
desire simply does not exist for Burke, but if it did, its passions would
seem to be allied with sublimity. For what it is worth, a few pages before
the beginning of Part Three, Burke notes that bitter tastes and stenches,
including "the bitter apples of Sodom," induce "ideas suitable to a sublime description" (78).

My second example comes from Hegel's discussion of Greek statuary
art in his *Aesthetics*. For Hegel, Greek art supremely embodies the ideal
of the beautiful in which visible form and a richly determined and indi-
vidualized consciousness harmoniously combine. In a section entitled "Particular Aspects of the Ideal From in Sculpture," he undertakes to itemize
those formal qualities of face and body that elevate Greek art to its ideal
status. Before beginning, however, he discharges an intellectual debt:

> If we turn now to consider in more detail the chief features of importance
> in connection with ideal sculptural form, we will follow Winkelmann in the
> main; with the greatest insight and felicity he has described the particular
> forms and the way they were treated and developed by Greek artists until
> they count as the sculptural ideal. Their liveliness, this deliquescence, eludes
> the categories of the Understanding which cannot grasp the particular here
> or get to the root of it as it can in architecture [mathematically]. (727)[4]

Hegel borrows liberally from the catalogue of statuary facial features and
body parts in Winkelmann's *History of Ancient Art* (1765), though his
analysis rarely follows his predecessor's. The distinctive qualities of Greek
art that Hegel claims to learn through Winkelmann is "their liveliness,
this deliquescence" (*Die Lebendigheit, dies Zerfliessende*). Both Hegel and
Winkelmann distinguish Greek statues from their Egyptian forerunners
on these grounds. But "deliquescence" also glances at the homoerotic
element in Winkelmann's work. The *History of Ancient Art* elevates the
figure of the eighteenth-century castrato to a classical ideal, reflecting
Winkelmann's sexual interest in the castrati he consorted with in Rome.[5]
What Winkelmann valued aesthetically in the bodies of castrati and of
youths was an indeterminacy of line (and of gender) that distinguished

them from the hard outlines of adult male figures. "Here however in the great unity of youthful forms, the outlines themselves imperceptibly flow one into the other" (*unmerklich eine in die andere fliessen*).[6] The "deliquescence" (*Zerfliessen*) of which Hegel takes note is therefore for Winkelmann the flowing (*fliessen*) of lines in the androgynous and attractive figure of the male youth.

I do not wish to claim, however, that in praising Winkelmann Hegel either assumes or endorses the homoerotic strains in the latter's work. On the contrary, Hegel's analysis systematically dampens the sensuous elements in Winkelmann's descriptions. Moreover, this neutralization is, I would argue, elevated to a kind of thematic status when Hegel discusses the eyes of Greek statues. Hegel begins this discussion by insisting that Greeks painted in the eyes of statues only as an exception, and that the blankness of the eye is therefore a deliberate norm. He gives several reasons, of which two are pertinent here. First, a man's

> glance is what is most full of his soul, the concentration of his inmost personality and being. . . . But in sculpture [as opposed to painting] the sphere of the artist is neither the inner feeling of the soul, the concentration of the whole man into the one simple self which appears in the glance as this ultimate point of illumination, nor with the personality diffused in the complications of the external world. Sculpture has as its aim the entirety of the external form over which it must disperse the soul, and it must present it in this variety, and therefore it is not allowed to bring back this variety to one simple soulful point and the momentary glance of the eye. (73)

In other words, Greek statues must lack a seeing eye because the expression of soul must be distributed over the entirety of their form. Second, "the eye looks out into the external world; . . . But the genuine sculptural figure is precisely withdrawn from this link with external things and is immersed in the substantial nature of its spiritual content, independent in itself, not dispersed in or complicated by anything else" (732–33). The statue is therefore blind because it looks inward rather than outward; it "sees" only its withdrawn spiritual content and not the external world.

This theme of blindness recurs indirectly when Hegel turns to the question of nude and draped forms in Greek sculpture. The Greeks, claims Hegel, valued personal individuality and therefore respected the bare human figure because it is "the freest and most beautiful one. In this

sense of course they discarded that shame or modesty which forbids the
purely human body to be seen, and they did this, not from indifference
to the spiritual, but from indifference to purely sensual desire, for the
sake of beauty alone" (744). Of course, as Hegel notes, the Greeks
sculpted primarily male figures nude. The "indifference to purely sensual
desire" (*Gleichgültigkeit gegen das nur Sinnliche der Begierde*)[7] that allows
aesthetic appreciation of the male body thus recalls Burke's negation of
homoerotic desire in his definition of beauty. But while Burke denies the
very existence of such desire, Hegel insists rather that the Greeks do not
care for it—they abstain from desiring this desire. To put it differently,
the desire is there, but Greek eyes do not see it, and this not-seeing
defines the aesthetic quality of their vision. Moreover, while describing
the Greeks themselves as spectators, Hegel's remarks clarify in retrospect
the blindness of Greek statues. For what these statues (like the Greeks
who sculpted them) do not see is sensual desire, specifically male homoerotic desire. Following a classically Freudian formula, then, we may say
that blindness takes the place in Hegel that castration occupied in
Winkelmann. The not-seeing of Greek statues is their way of incorporating the neutralization of desire that characterizes not only the Greeks
but the subject of aesthetic contemplation more generally. The blind eyes
of Greek statues teach the spectator in turn a blindness with respect to
merely sensual content. But this (partial) negation of the visual in Greek
art also recalls the more thoroughgoing annihilation of images that characterized the Hebraic sublime in Hegel. Greek beauty ascends to the spiritual, and it does so by blotting out the merely sensual, thus retaining a
faint echo of its sublime precursor even as it celebrates the image. Where
St. Paul saw Greek statues as fomenting homosexuality by turning the
Greeks away from the sublime God, then, Hegel wields the sublime as a
way of cordoning Greek beauty off from Greek homosexuality.

These examples provide nothing more than an initial matrix for
this study. Aesthetic theory will play no great role in the chapters that follow. Nevertheless, Wilde, Freud, and Lacan share both an awareness of,
and a subversive intent toward, the tradition of philosophical aesthetics.
And Shakespeare constructs in his Sonnets an art that formulates—and
then shifts—its own aesthetic principles as it proceeds. All four writers
reflect in original ways upon the role of sexual desire in art (and art in
sexual desire), and all four do so by conjoining the unlikely categories of
sodomy and the sublime.

Before proceeding, however, I want to make clear what I do and do not hope to accomplish. Despite my book's subtitle, I have relatively little to say directly on the topic of sodomy, and not a great deal more to say on the topic of the sublime. Much of the interesting recent work on sodomy in the early modern period has involved opening the concept up to include its associations with nonsexual phenomena such as witchcraft, treason, heresy, and so on. But this larger penumbra of cultural meanings simply doesn't come into play in the specific tradition I address here. This is a book not about sodomy as such but about the way it is constructed by a specific, post-Pauline tradition. My treatment of sodomy is determined in large part by the fact that I focus on literary and theoretical texts, not on the legal arguments and the medical and theological treatises on which historians of sexuality have tended to base their work. In all the writings I address, sodomy is invoked either fleetingly or implicitly. Indeed, it constitutes a kind of empty hole in discourse, about which nothing directly *can* be said. This is one of its points of contact with the sublime. In any case, both sodomy and the sublime, taken separately, are topics that have generated abundant commentary and scholarship in recent years. My contribution, as I see it, is to draw previously unnoticed connections between the two. It is only natural, then, that I should focus on mediating terms, of which sublimation is the most important for my purposes.

Perhaps it is only a restatement of the previous paragraph to say that, while I hope this work will be of interest to queer theorists and historians of sexuality, I consider it to be primarily concerned with literary criticism and aesthetics. It would be an exaggeration to say that this is a book about art, not life. But it is more about literary constructions of the sexual than it is about the history of sexuality. Moreover, the specific lineage of writers I construct will be a puzzling and even troubling one, since it conjoins a foundational homophobe (St. Paul), a foundational homosexual (Oscar Wilde), the writer of the world's most renowned same-sex love sonnets, and two of the most influential figures in psychoanalysis, a discourse and practice that have had a history of enforcing heteronormativity. This strange constellation of writers argues for the continuing and even generative presence of phobic strains in the construction of a "canonical" homosexuality—that is, same-sex desire as represented by some central texts and writers of the literary canon. I think it is fair to say that Shakespeare, Wilde, Freud, and Lacan all struggle with St. Paul, or with the tradition to which he gives rise, and that they manage to wrest something unexpected and even delightfully perverse from his dour moralizing. But it is true at the same time that Paul exerts an irresistible pressure despite the twistings and turnings to which he is subjected. And he does so not merely through the dead weight of cultural tradition but because his disagreeable fulminations also display a brilliance that almost invites revision. As a result of the fascination he exerts, later writers end up saying things that they might not be expected (or even wanted) to say.

Although the four figures on whom I focus have been arranged in chronological order, and some later writers even refer to earlier ones, nothing so coherent as a history emerges from the series I present. If anything, what I uncover is a compulsion to repeat a culturally primal scene. This is not a book about the emergence of modern homosexual identity, in part because the instances of sodomy I examine are, almost as often as not, heterosexual. But also in part because this a book about the ways in which an older, sodomitical thematic persists even into the modern regime of sexual identities, when its cultural supports might seem to have fallen away.

CHAPTER ONE

Shakespeare's Perfume

Given his many forays into the realms of art and literature, Freud shows a surprising lack of interest in the love lyric. Surprising, because such poetry would seem to offer an obvious point of connection between eros and art. Perhaps too obvious. Not only is the Freudian hermeneutic drawn more to covert or occulted expressions of sexuality, but Freud's theory of art as *sublimated* desire ascribes a certain "coolness" or desexualized quality to the artwork. The love poem, a literary form which not only takes sexual desire as its explicit content but also frequently adopts a rhetoric of seduction, lacks both the representational and the libidinal distance that a Freudian theory of art seems, if not exactly to require, then at least to prefer. The love lyric conjoins sex and art in so blatant a way as to be, for Freud at least, apparently devoid of interest.

Yet in the Petrarchan tradition, which includes Shakespeare's sonnets, love poetry often represents a form of sexual desire which is both idealized and sublimated.[1] Likewise the courtly love lyric, in which the beloved is elevated to an object of almost religious veneration, offers Jacques Lacan a privileged point of entry for his own distinctive theory of sublimation. (Both Freud's and Lacan's theories of sublimation will be addressed in later chapters of this book.)

In the case of Shakespeare's sonnets, a sublimating interpretation has been both encouraged and complicated by the fact that most of the sequence's poems are addressed to a young man. The most famous—and, I will argue—the most profound instance of such an interpretation occurs in Oscar Wilde's novella *The Portrait of Mr. W.H.* Wilde's fictional critic Cyril Graham depicts Shakespeare as the victim of a largely desexualized but still somewhat intoxicating fascination with the beauty and personality of the man whom Graham "identifies" as a young actor named Willie Hughes.[2] Graham goes on to argue that not only Shakespeare's sonnets but "the essentially male culture of the English Renaissance"

(194)³ derives much of its inspiration from Ficino's translation of Plato's *Symposium*, which extols a decorporealized love between men. "There was a kind of mystic transference of the expressions of the physical sphere to a sphere that was spiritual, that was removed from gross bodily appetite, and in which the soul was Lord" (185).

Wilde's sublimating interpretation of the sonnets has found answering echoes among critics from G. Wilson Knight to W. H. Auden to Joel Fineman.⁴ More recently, however, and particularly at the hands of gay criticism and queer theory, sublimating interpretations of the Sonnets have come under severe critical scrutiny. The Freudian associations of the term "sublimation" have rendered it doubly suspect, as being both ahistorical and tainted by its association with a discourse that has sometimes classed homosexuality as pathological. Moreover, the postulate of a sublimated homosexuality in the Sonnets has (with some reason) been seen as a strategy for installing an aestheticized, desexualized, and therefore relatively sanitized and "acceptable" version of same-sex passion that would allow homophobic readers of the Sonnets to acknowledge the unavoidable fact of homosexual desire while ignoring its more earthy and direct expressions.⁵

This last objection strikes me as the most significant of the three. English Petrarchanism, starting with Thomas Wyatt, has always accommodated a strongly anti-idealizing strain. Shakespeare's sonnets to the young man combine a rhetoric of sublimation with an exuberantly bawdy taste for sexual wordplay.⁶ Any theory of sublimation that either ignores or is embarrassed by the poems' repeated references to same-sex *practices* as well as desires will thus be guilty of both homophobia and simple inaccuracy. Wilde, it should be said, balanced his sublimating interpretation of the Sonnets with intimations of things forbidden. Cyril Graham is careful to mention "critics, like Hallam, who had regretted that the Sonnets had even been written, who had seen in them something dangerous, something unlawful even" (186–87). And he admits to being "almost afraid to turn the key that unlocks the mystery of the poet's heart" (160). Wilde will not and cannot name this secret, of course, but he takes pains to communicate its presence to the reader, as both the antithesis of and the counterpart to sublimated desire. Wilde's invocation of sodomy only as the unnameable secret is, as we shall see in a later chapter, dictated by motives other than simple prudence. The rhetoric of the unspeakable is not merely a means of avoidance or self-protection but a positive strategy with both political and aesthetic dimensions. In any case, Wilde's ability to find in the Sonnets both a legitimate, because sublimated, form of same-sex desire *and* the unspeakable crime of sodomy is not a simple contradiction. It results, rather, from careful reading of the Sonnets' own rhetoric of sublimation.

In this chapter I shall argue that Shakespeare's Sonnets contain not only a rhetoric but what one might go so far as to call a "theory" of sublimation, and that such a theory will enable us to pass from a merely thematic handling of male same-sex desire to the aesthetic principles that govern the form of the Sonnets. It will also, I believe, answer the charges of ahistoricism by positing sublimation not as a way of processing a non-historical essence called "homosexual desire" but as a discourse that helps to *produce* such desire in a culturally and historically specific way.

My initial focus will be that subsequence of poems, beginning with the first sonnet and usually but not always taken as ending with the seventeenth, known as the "procreation sonnets." These poems might seem to offer a counterintuitive starting point. For one thing, in counseling the young man to reproduce, they promote a distinctly nonsublimated form of sexual activity. For another, in counseling him to take a wife, or at least a mistress, they offer a curiously mediated and indirect form of same-sex desire. It is nevertheless these sonnets that formulate, in an especially striking and visible way, a poetics of sublimation. And they do so in a manner that defines the nature of same-sex desire for the entire sequence of poems to the young man.

Typical of the procreation sonnets in many respects is number 5:

Those hours that with gentle work did frame
The lovely gaze where every eye doth dwell
Will play the tyrants to the very same
And that unfair which fairly doth excel:
For never-resting time leads summer on
To hideous winter and confounds him there,
Sap checked with frost and lusty leaves quite gone,
Beauty o'ersnowed and bareness everywhere.
Then were not summer's distillation left
A liquid pris'ner pent in walls of glass,
Beauty's effect with beauty were bereft,
Nor it nor no remembrance what it was.
　　But flow'rs distilled, though they with winter meet,
　　Leese but their show, their substance still lives sweet.

Like many of the procreation sonnets, this one employs a turn on the familiar *carpe diem* argument: since time will soon ruin your beauty, it cautions, best to have sex now. Only in this case, have sex with someone other than me—with a woman who will bear your child. Somehow the sonneteer's rhetoric of seduction has gotten twisted in the direction of family values. Indeed, the sense of imminent demise that pervades the poem works less to whip up a desperate sexual longing than to mortify desire into something merely prudent. It makes sex seem as exciting as putting up preserves.

The poem's most interesting and (not incidentally) most elegiacally beautiful lines introduce the image of the perfume bottle. But while this metaphor bolsters the poem's longing for a beauty that transcends death, it fits somewhat awkwardly with its supposed tenor. In the translation from a child, to semen in a womb, to perfume in a bottle, something has been lost, and that something is life. The glass bottle is, to begin with, a conspicuously sterile and inorganic image for the womb. It *contains* the vital fluid, but does not nourish or quicken it. Its beauty is therefore static—not so much the transcendence as the incorporation of death. It turns birth into stillbirth.

But if the image of perfume and glass is vastly ill-suited to its stated purpose of figuring sexual procreation, it is, as more than one critic has noticed, perfectly suited to another, implied purpose: that of figuring *poetic* procreation.[7] The diminutive, unchanging perfection of the perfume bottle thus represents not a baby but a sonnet. The glass womb is the male womb of Shakespearean verse,[8] in which the young man's essence will be perpetuated, not as another living and therefore perishable blossom but rather as eternal though static lines of poetry.

This particular substitution is in itself neither novel nor surprising. Its interest, from my perspective, is that it makes Sonnet 5 into a tiny treatise on poetic sublimation. What I mean by this is that Shakespeare's image of the perfume bottle takes the commonplace but mysterious process whereby the father's sexual substance produces a baby, and puts in its place the even more mysterious process whereby the young man's sexual substance—his semen—is distilled into poetry. Sonnet 5 seems to offer a curiously material demonstration, even before the fact, of the Freudian thesis that sexual desire can be sublimated into art.

Both Shakespearean and Freudian sublimation find their origin in older traditions of medical and alchemical literature, especially the latter.

Two of alchemy's principal refining processes were distillation, or the evaporation and recondensation of liquids, and sublimation, or the evaporation and recondensation of solids. Both aimed at separating and elevating a purer and more spiritualized substance from a grosser and more corporeal one. Nicolas Flamel, a medieval French alchemist whose works were translated into English in 1624, writes:

> Note therefore, that this separation, division, and sublimation, is without doubt the *key* of the whole worke. After the putrefaction, then, and dissolution of these *Bodies*, our *Bodies* doe lift themselves up to the surface of the dissolving water, in the colour of *whitenesse*, and this *whitenesse* is *life*; ... which separateth the subtile from the thicke, and the pure from the impure, lifting up by little and little the subtile part of the *Body*, from the dregs, untill all the pure be separated and lifted up: And in this is our *Philosophicall* and natural sublimation fulfilled: And in this *whitenesse* is the soule infused into the *Body*, that is, the mineral vertue, which is more subtile than *fire*, being indeed the true quintessence and life, which desireth to bee borne, and to put off the grosse earthly *faeces*, which it hath taken from the *Menstruous* and corrupt place of his origin.[9]

Alchemical sublimation thus produces two substances: a purified and spiritualized essence and, separated from this, a fecal discharge or remainder. In turning solid to gas, and gas back to solid, sublimation was seen as transforming body to spirit and spirit to body. The goal was not a separation of spirit *from* matter but a reconciliation of spirit *with* a purified matter:[10] hence the sublimate was often compared to an infant emerging from the womb or to Christ's resurrected body.[11] The fecal remainder, by contrast, was associated variously with earth, with menses, with putrefaction, and with death. Flamel writes of this discharge or remainder that "it stincks, and gives a smell like the odour of *graves* filled with rottennesse, and with bodies as yet charged with their naturall moysture."[12] It is also, not incidentally, associated with the female body. Flamel elsewhere describes sublimation as the process of eliminating "the dark moiste dominion of the *woman*."[13] Sublimation is thus not only a purifying but a defeminizing process, qualities that will persist when the concept is adopted by Freud.

Returning to Sonnet 5, we can see how the tropes of alchemical sublimation serve to imagine a masculinized, poetic birth. The metaphor of glass bottle as womb was already widespread in alchemical literature before Shakespeare borrows it here. Moreover, male semen resembles the alchemical quintessence not only in its masculinity and its white color, but because Renaissance medicine already conceived of semen as a distillation and purification of the blood. I am not arguing that the images of Sonnet 5 are specifically alchemical in origin, although Shakespeare's sonnets make occasional explicit reference to alchemy. Obviously, the direct subject matter here is perfume-making. Rather I am arguing that discourses such as alchemy, medicine, and even perfume-making shared a common figural vocabulary of sublimation.

Our brief survey of alchemy immediately reveals something crucial about Sonnet 5: the poem depicts only the perfume as distillate, while the waste matter or remainder of distillation has disappeared. Shakespeare's imagery of distillation is thus, itself, distilled or purified. The effects of this may become clearer when set against another image of distilled perfume, this one occurring in John Donne's eighth elegy, "The Comparison." Donne's poem consists of a series of contrasting descriptions pitting the speaker's own, beautiful mistress against the putatively repulsive mistress of a male friend. It begins thus:

> As the sweet sweat of roses in a still,
> As that which from chafed musk cat's pores doth trill,
> As th'almighty balm of th'early east,
> Such are the sweat drops of my mistress' breast.
> And on her neck her skin such lustre sets,
> They are no sweat drops but pearl carcanets.
> Rank sweaty froth thy mistress' brow defiles,
> Like spermatic issue of ripe menstruous boils,
> Or like that scum, which by need's lawless law
> Enforced, Sanserra's starved men did draw
> From parboiled shoes, and boots, and all the rest
> Which were with any sovereign fatness blessed,
> And like vile lying stones in saffroned tin,
> Or warts, or weals, they hang upon her skin. (1–14)[14]

It is no coincidence that the first set of comparisons takes up fourteen lines, for despite the rhyming couplets this is clearly an anti-sonnet. Inversion of structure (an opening sestet followed by an octave) announces a thematic inversion of Petrarchanism, the latter's presence signaled once again by imagery of distillation. But if Donne grotesquely parodies a sublimating rhetoric, he does so (paradoxically) not by negating it but by completing it—that is to say, by portraying not only the distillate but the remainder as well. For Donne, something like alchemical separation produces two contrasting women: one the traditionally idealized Petrarchan mistress, the other a repulsive mass of scum and sores. These are, of course, simply the two halves of the fantasized diptych known as Woman, seen here simultaneously and anamorphically rather than (as in Spenser's Duessa, for example) sequentially.

Things aren't so simple, however, for the strain of sublimation imprints itself even on the first, "pure" mistress. The opening comparison, "As the sweet *sweat* of roses," exhibits a slightly oxymoronic stress that bursts forth in the grotesque second line. The very fact of choosing sweat for his first point of comparison—a kind of bodily distillate, to be sure, but one of necessarily compromised purity—indicates the limits of sublimation when the poetic subject is woman.

Yet the threat of contamination runs not only between the two women, but between woman and man. The grotesque qualities of the "other" mistress, after all, derive both here and elsewhere in the poem from a disturbing admixture of masculinity, visible in the "spermatic issue" and in the image of Sanserra's men boiling their shoes. What the sublimating movement of "The Comparison" actually hopes to separate—and in the end, does separate—is not one woman from another, but woman from man. The poem ends by exhorting the friend to abandon his mistress and (in a slightly more covert vein) to take Donne himself as an erotic substitute.[15] The grotesque hermaphroditism of the "other" mistress is finally resolved, then, not by purging her of the offending masculinity, but by purging the masculinity of her. In the final irony of the poem, the masculine "remainder" is transubstantiated and saved as sublimate while even the idealized, Petrarchan woman is abjected as waste matter.

In Shakespeare's sonnets, the young man is sometimes depicted as sublimate, sometimes as sublimating agent—both product and radiant source of alchemical refinement.[16] The waste remainder is associated primarily (though not exclusively) with woman, as in Donne. In fact, Shakespeare's Dark Lady embodies every aspect of what Nicholas Flamel calls the "dark moist dominion of woman."[17] But if the young man serves as the sublimated opposite of the Dark Lady, this is not to say that he is free of feminine attributes. Indeed, Sonnet 20 dwells at length on the young man's androgyny, though this "master mistress" is depicted as an even purer version of the idealized Petrarchan mistress. In Sonnet 5,

intimations of femininity surround the perfume bottle. Donne, for
instance, writes of perfume: "By thee, the greatest stain to man's estate/
Falls on us, to be called effeminate" (Elegy 4, 61–62). Moreover, the distilling of perfume from flowers is used elsewhere in Shakespeare as a
metaphor for *female* sexual pleasure.[18] Of course, perfume would seem to
evoke the sweet Petrarchan mistress (as in Sonnet 20) and not her
abjected "other." Yet in the early modern period perfume was frequently
used to cover the smells of unwashed or diseased bodies. Donne, typically, expresses what Shakespeare represses. His fourth elegy apostro-
phizes perfume in the following terms:

> Base excrement of earth, which dost confound
> Sense, from distinguishing the sick from sound;
> By thee the silly amorous sucks his death
> By drawing in a leprous harlot's breath. (57–60)

It is not my intention to claim that the perfume bottle of Sonnet 5
evokes all these things; the miracle is rather that it doesn't. Shakespeare's
crystal flask does not harbor a Baudelairean "parfum corrumpu." Perhaps this is because it exists primarily as a visual rather than an olfactory
object, and so suspends or cancels the connections on which Donne
dwells. Trapped within its bottle, the perfume is prevented from releas-
ing its associative as well as its floral bouquet. Instead, the image achieves
a kind of untroubled luminescence in which the crystalline enclosure of
the bottle signifies, among other things, its isolation from all that was
abjected to produce its contents. A manifestation of pure *claritas*, Shakespeare's perfume bottle is a distant ancestor of the snowy, aseptic bowl in
Wallace Stevens's "The Poems of Our Climate." The bottle's walls of glass
are visually transparent but semiotically opaque; they reduce the image
to mere seeming or appearance rather than meaning.

But while the sublimating rhetoric of Sonnet 5 leaves no residue, it
does offer a faint commemoration of the labor needed to expel it. The
image of the perfume as a "prisoner pent" suggests a latent dynamism
that threatens the visual repose of the image—indeed, threatens it from
within. This one detail causes the image to vibrate with the energy of
everything it tries to exclude. By "everything," as we have seen, I mean in
part "woman." But as we shall see next, I also mean in part "sodomy."

* * *

"Procreation sonnet" has become such a convenient term for the opening seventeen poems of the Quarto sequence, it trips so easily from the
tongue, that one is prone to overlook how very odd a thing a sonnet on
procreation is. In every respect it seems to violate the sexual canons of a
form traditionally devoted to idealized worship on the one hand and lib-
ertine seduction on the other. The procreation sonnet at once charts a
third option and splits the difference between the first two, since it counsels sex in the name of reproductive duty—that is to say, for a purpose
other than that of sexual pleasure itself.

But while they enjoin childbearing, the procreation sonnets
strangely evacuate the content of this duty. First, as Joseph Pequigney
notes, they deprive themselves of possible arguments by inexplicably fail-
ing to allude to the young man's noble birth: "They might easily have
done so; they might have urged his responsibility to his family, to hand
on a great name, to enable the passage of a title or property along blood-
lines, to provide for the maintenance of an ancestral house."[19] Second,
they refrain from mentioning any divine injunctions to be fruitful and
multiply.[20] So the "duty" of procreation, whatever it may be, stems neither from God nor from the social order. Then why reproduce? The very
first lines of sonnet 1 say why:

> From fairest creatures we desire increase,
> That thereby beauty's rose might never die,
> But as the riper should by time decease,
> His tender heir might bear his memory. (1–4)

Reproduction is, in the first instance, an *aesthetic* duty; its purpose and
aim is the perpetuation of the beautiful. Moreover, as we learn in Sonnet
11, Nature has granted beautiful creatures a reproductive advantage with
just this aim in mind:

> Let those whom nature hath not made for store,
> Harsh, featureless, and rude, barrenly perish.
> Look whom she best endowed, she gave the more;
> Which bounteous gift thou shouldst in bounty cherish.
>   She carved thee for her seal, and meant thereby
>   Thou shouldst print more, not let that copy die. (9–14)

In reproducing, the young man will obey natural law; to this point,
Shakespeare's argument appears quite orthodox. But by redefining the

aim of that law so radically, the procreation sonnets engage, as we shall see, in a theologically subversive form of aestheticism.

This redefinition will, moreover, engage the problem of sodomy. For in the very process of endorsing a licit, reproductive sexuality, the procreation sonnets employ a range of figures that mimic, and in some cases may derive from, theological condemnations of sodomy. If at times these sonnets covertly endorse or propose sodomitical practices, they also constitute a distinctive sexual aesthetic precisely by negating, expelling, or purging sodomy.

One way in which they do so is by repeatedly advising the young man on the proper "use" of his semen. In Sonnet 4, which tries to dissuade the young man from masturbation, variations on the word "use" ("abuse," "usurer," "use," "unused," "used") occur five times. Sonnet 6 repeats Sonnet 4's contrast between the procreative "use" of semen and "forbidden usury" (5). As Mark Jordan shows in his book *The Invention of Sodomy in Christian Theology*, medieval theologians often defined sodomy not as a forbidden form of sexual desire or as an excessive form of pleasure or even as a specifically same-sex practice but simply as a misuse of semen for anything—including male masturbation—that does not serve to fulfil its reproductive potential. Albertus Magnus even goes so far as to state that *female* masturbation is not necessarily sinful since it does not entail a waste of male seed.[21] In Thomas Aquinas, distinctions between legitimate and sodomitical sex turn entirely on the proper or improper "use" (*usus*) of the seed, a vocabulary that informs Shakespeare's procreation sonnets as well.[22] Likewise, the conception of sodomy as usury derives from medieval sources. Dante puts sodomites and usurers in the same circle of hell. In urging the proper "use" of the young man's semen, the procreation sonnets thus engage a theological discourse that opposes such use to sodomitical "abuse" or "usury." Yet even as they employ a theologically derived vocabulary, and do so precisely to invoke the specter of sodomy, the sonnets never adopt a tone of theological condemnation. Indeed, the sonnets undermine the theological concept of "use" by twisting that term, as we have seen, in a purely aesthetic direction. For Shakespeare, as opposed to Aquinas or Albertus Magnus, the proper "use" of semen involves not the creation of life as such but the creation of beauty.

Theological distinctions between the use and sodomitical abuse of semen frequently invoked a supplementary distinction between the female womb as semen's "proper vessel" and the anus (male or female) as an "improper vessel." The proper vessel fulfils the semen's procreative potential while the improper vessel wastes it. To borrow Shakespeare's vocabulary in Sonnet 3, the latter is semen's "tomb" rather than its "womb." I believe that by depicting the womb as a "vial" Sonnets 5 and 6 invoke something very like this medieval figure and its context. Yet in doing so the sonnets transform it just as they did the term "use"—by aestheticizing it. For, as we have seen, the perfume bottle fails as metaphor precisely by evacuating *life* in favor of art. Shakespeare thus summons up the image of the proper vessel in order to pervert it. Instead of abandoning the proper for an officially improper vessel, he makes the proper vessel itself improper by substituting an aesthetic function for a reproductive one. In effect, he refashions the theologians' vessel of birth into something like an ornate vase or a crystal vial, beautiful but barren objects that contain only poetic *claritas*.

From this moment of conversion or transformation, something one might call Shakespearean homosexuality emerges. It is not identical with sodomy but results, rather, from aestheticizing the theological categories that construct sodomy. Here I will venture a preliminary formula: *Shakespearean homosexuality is the aesthetic sublimate of sodomy*. This way of putting it reverses the terms of Freudian sublimation, since, instead of regarding art as the displacement of sexual aims, it posits Shakespearean homosexuality as itself a product or effect of the aesthetic. In this sense, the thesis championed by readers from Wilde to Auden to Fineman— that Shakespearean homosexuality is idealized or sublimated—seems exactly right. The sublimating rhetoric of the sonnets separates out an impeccably refined and aestheticized form of desire from a sodomitical discourse that is then abjected as fecal remainder. This remainder is not, however, expelled to a space outside the poems, but is rather relegated to a nonspace *within* the poems. That is to say, it abides in the half-light of wordplay, implication, and insinuation. Sodomy subsists as the speaking of the unspeakable, as the *topos* of the inexpressible or unnameable. Perhaps it is more correct, then, to identify Shakespearean homosexuality with both sublimate *and* remainder, or indeed with the very separation that produces this double product. The Shakespearean sonnet gives off a perfume that contains just the slightest hint of feces.

But while Shakespeare's sublimating rhetoric produces a significant poetic achievement, it does so at some cost. For what the division into spiritualized friendship and obscene wordplay evacuates is precisely the middle space of eros. Shakespeare's sacrifice may become clearer when the Sonnets are contrasted with another piece of homoerotic verse from roughly the same period: Richard Barnfield's *The Affectionate Shepherd*:

> O would to God (so might I have my fee)
> My lips were honey, and thy mouth a Bee.
>
> Then shouldst thou sucke my sweet and my faire flower
> That now is ripe, and full of honey-berries:
> Then would I leade thee to my pleasant Bower
> Fild full of Grapes, of Mulberries and Cherries;
>   Then shouldst thou be my Waspe or else my Bee,
>   I would thy hive, and thou my honey bee.[23]

Shakespeare's sonnets (and, for the most part, the plays) produce nothing like the erotic concreteness of such verse. Indeed, the first 126 sonnets evacuate fleshly desire to the point that they do not even allow the reader to visualize the young man. Shakespeare never shares even those qualities such as hair and eye color that typify the poetic blazon, although we learn in Sonnet 20 that the young man's appearance is androgynous. One of the fundamental ironies of Wilde's *Portrait of Mr. W.H.*, then, is that Shakespeare provides no directions for such a portrait. The sublimating logic of the first 126 sonnets drains their poetic subject of all corporeal specificity, leaving only a glassy, transparent vehicle of poetic comparison: the young man as perfume bottle.

* * *

We now arrive at a question that we will pose and repose throughout this book: what is the link between sublimation, a psychoanalytic (and alchemical) concept, and the sublime, a theological and aesthetic one? The way to negotiate this crossing in Sonnet 5 is far from obvious. Certainly, the poem does not ascend to anything recognizable as an aesthetics of the sublime; the image of the perfume bottle is, rather, beautiful, and may even emblematize the sonnets' fidelity to an aesthetics of the beautiful. In this section, then, I want to address the problem of the sublime directly, in the hope of reconciling it with Shakespeare's poetics of sublimation.

My starting point here will be chapter one of Paul's Epistle to the Romans. Having divided the world into Jews and gentiles, Paul then identifies idolatry as the defining sin of the gentiles, and especially of the Greeks:

18 For the wrath of God is revealed from heaven against all ungodliness and unrighteousness of men, who hold the truth in unrighteousness;
19 Because that which may be known of God is manifest in them; for God hath showed it unto them.
20 For the invisible things of him from the creation of the world are clearly seen, being understood by the things that are made, even his eternal power and Godhead; so that they are without excuse.
21 Because that, when they knew God, they glorified him not as God, neither were thankful; but became vain in their imaginations, and their foolish heart was darkened.
22 Professing themselves to be wise, they became fools,
23 And changed the glory of the uncorruptible God into an image made like to corruptible man, and to birds, and four-footed beasts, and creeping things.
24 Wherefore God gave them up to uncleanness, through the lusts of their own hearts, to dishonor their own bodies between themselves:
25 Who changed the truth of God into a lie, and worshipped and served the creature more than the Creator, who is blessed forever. Amen.
26 For this cause God gave them up unto vile affections: for even their women did change the natural use into that which is against nature:
27 And likewise also the men, leaving the natural use of the woman, burned in their lust one toward another; men with men working that which is unseemly, and receiving in themselves that recompense of their error which was meet. (KJV)

This passage is interesting to me on several counts. First, Paul defines Greek culture by homosexuality on the one hand and an unhealthy addiction to statues on the other. But as in Shakespeare, it is an excess of the aesthetic, one might say, that gives rise to homosexuality, rather than homosexuality that finds its sexual desire sublimed into art. Second, by specifying homosexuality as the punishment for idolatry, Paul situates it in relation to the unrepresentability of God, and hence in relation to what would later be called the sublime.

The logic by which Paul connects homosexuality and idolatry is not immediately apparent, but we can elaborate it by noticing that this passage is constructed around three occurrences of the Greek verb *(met)ellaxan* or "exchange." Because the Greeks have exchanged the unrepresentable God for visible, created things (representations of nature), they are forced to exchange the "natural" objects of desire for unnatural ones. But this means that homosexuality, as a failure of natural vision, mimics that transcendence of nature which the Greeks otherwise fail to achieve. In other words, homosexuality is the equivalent, as well as the opposite, of sublime transcendence.

The story of Sodom and Gomorrah in Genesis 19 exhibits similar traits. When the inhabitants of Sodom attempt to break down Lot's door and ravish the angels within, they are blinded by a bright light, and this failure of vision mockingly repeats their refusal to recognize the invisible God and his messengers. The blinding light in the doorway, moreover, presages the consuming fires that will destroy Sodom in a sublime act of divine de-creation. These flames, as a direct manifestation of godhead, are also under a visual prohibition, as Lot's wife learns the hard way.[24] Thus the Sodom story likewise connects homosexuality, loss or cancellation of vision, and the sublime transcendence of God. (Chapter 5 of Peter Martyr's *Book of Gomorrah* articulates Romans 1 and Genesis 19 on all three of these counts.)[25]

What that same Peter Martyr will be the first to call "sodomy"[26] thus occupies an ambiguous relation to the sublime God, at once his demonic opposite and his troubling equivalent. Nowhere is this clearer than in sodomy's status as the unnameable or unspeakable vice, from whose utterance even God's angels will flee. For this prohibition on speech makes sodomy the obscene counterpart to the Tetragrammaton, or the unspeakable name of God.[27] John Bale's Protestant morality play, *The Three Laws of Nature, Moses, and Christ* (1538), pairs the allegorical characters Sodomy and Idolatry, thus betraying the influence of Romans 1 and its elaboration by Thomas Aquinas. When the character Infidelity conjures up this devilish pair, he does so as follows: "By Tetragrammaton, / I charge ye, apere anon, / And come out of the darke."[28] Not only are Sodomy and Idolatry invoked by the divine Tetragrammaton, but in being ordered to "come out of the dark," they are depicted as inhabitants of a hidden space that resists representation. Sodomy is, here as elsewhere, a devilish subspecies of the sublime.

This connection between sodomy and sublimity is crucial, I believe, to Shakespeare's Sonnets—not because the Sonnets (at least those to the young man) embrace either term but because they avoid both, and in so doing define their own aesthetic.[29] Nowhere does this appear more clearly than in the much-discussed Sonnet 20:

A woman's face, with Nature's own hand painted,
Hast thou, the master-mistress of my passion—
A woman's gentle heart, but not acquainted
With shifting change, as is false women's fashion;
An eye more bright than theirs, less false in rolling,
Gilding the object whereupon it gazeth;
A man in hue, all hues in his controlling,
Which steals men's eyes and women's souls amazeth.
And for a woman wert thou first created,
Till nature as she wrought thee fell a-doting,
And by addition me of thee defeated,
By adding one thing to my purpose nothing.
But since she pricked thee out for women's pleasure,
Mine be thy love, and thy love's use their treasure.

Most recent commentary on this sonnet has worked ingeniously to
undercut the apparent gesture of sexual renunciation in the poem's final
lines. I would like to focus rather on the figure of Nature, who occupies
almost as much of the poem as the young man. The image of Nature
fashioning human beings draws on long-standing medieval traditions of
the goddess Natura's double role as procreatrix and *vicaria dei* or vicar of
God.[30] Nature's apparent inattentiveness at this job is also not new, hark-
ing back to Prudentius[31] and Alan of Lille, although the myth of Pyg-
malion and Galatea may also hover in the background. As the procreative
deputy of God, Nature engages in an activity that at once recalls and
differs from divine creation. As Alan of Lille puts it in his *Anticlaudianus*,
"divinum creat ex nihilo, Natura caduca / procreat ex aliquo" II, 72–73)—
"the divine one creates from nothing, Nature breeds perishable things
from something."[32] Alan's phrasing is, I think, suggestive for Sonnet 20,
both in its play on "nothing" and "something," which presages line 12 of
Shakespeare's poem, and in contrasting Nature's procreation with the
sublime scene of God's *creatio ex nihilo*.

The odd thing about all scenes in which a mythological Nature fashions human beings is that real nature doesn't work that way. People originate as tiny embryos and grow into adulthood; they aren't sculpted as
fully grown creatures. Thus Shakespeare's scene of creation, in which
Nature molds adult forms, inevitably invokes God's fashioning of Adam
and Eve in the first chapter of Genesis.[33] I would even argue that the play
on "something" and "nothing" in line 12 is meant in part to recall God's
original creation of something (indeed, everything) out of nothing.

But, typically, the goddess Natura both invokes and negates this scene of divine creation. A nurturing mother steps in for the sublime father Jehovah, natural birth for the original scene of creation. The feminizing logic of this substitution goes so far as to hint at a rewriting of Genesis in which Adam is a kind of supplementary afterthought to Eve. Or perhaps Shakespeare even understands the biblical line "male and female created he them" in a manner similar to that of the rabbinical commentators (and Renaissance Platonists) who argued that God created a single androgyne, which he subsequently split in two.[34]

In any case, the strategy of this sonnet is to summon up a sublime scene of creation in order then to veil it, by which I mean to naturalize, feminize, and aestheticize it. Divine narrative gets reworked here in the same way that theological categories did in the procreation sonnets. And to similar ends, since sodomitical undertones clearly disturb Sonnet 20. By adding a penis to the half-finished woman, Nature simultaneously invokes the specter of sodomy and fends it off, at least if we accept the poem's surface argument that this penis stands definitively in the way of sexual contact.[35] But what the poem has thereby and perhaps even more importantly avoided is a divine injunction *against* sodomy. To put this in Lacanian terms, Sonnet 20 substitutes a real impediment for a symbolic prohibition. That is, instead of the sublime "Thou shalt not" of an angry God, what bars access to the young man is just a harmless if frustrating bit of flesh. A piece of nature fends off the daunting theological apparatus of anti-sodomy discourse, thus defining a safe space in which homoerotic desire may be harmlessly indulged. The psychoanalytic significance of the poem may be brought out by quoting the Lacanian theorist Slavoj Žižek as he comments not on Shakespeare's Sonnet 20 but on the infamous scene of discovery in Neil Jordan's film *The Crying Game*: "This scene of failed sexual encounter is structured as the exact inversion of the scene referred to by Freud as the primordial trauma of fetishism: the child's gaze, sliding down the female body towards the sexual organs, is shocked to find nothing where one expects to find something (a penis)—in the case of *The Crying Game*, the shock is caused when the eye finds *something* where it expected to find *nothing*."[36] Or, to put this in more Shakespearean terms, when it finds something to its purpose nothing. The effect, however, is the same as in the classical Freudian scene. For just as the threat of castration leads, in Freud's narrative of the Oedipus complex, to a suspension of sexual desire and paralysis of the phallus known as the latency period, so in Sonnet 20 the superfluous presence of the young man's penis renders the speaker's penis likewise superfluous, at least in regard to the young man. The speaker finds his sexual impulses blocked, and this pacifying of desire helps to constitute the young man as something more like an art object than a sexual object. Indeed, it turns him into something like the perfume bottle of Sonnet five, which is to say, the object of a sonnet.

In attempting to move from sublimation to the sublime, my argument may seem to have landed in a contradiction. For my analysis of Sonnet 5 emphasized the defeminizing aspects of Shakespearean sublimation, but my reading of Sonnet 20 insists on its feminizing of a masculine sublime. Even if there is a contradiction here, it is Shakespeare's rather than my own. But, I would claim, it is less a contradiction than a multiplication of strategies to effect the same end. For the two poems share this double aim: to invoke the threat of sodomy so as to expel or foreclose it, and to invoke a poetics of the sublime so as to reject it in favor of a poetics of the beautiful. Sodomy and sublimity are engaged and neutralized as a linked pair. While somewhat idealized, then, the young man does not attain the inhuman and terrifying loftiness of the Petrarchan mistress. This sublime height, and depth, are avoided because they are also the realm where sodomy and its divine punishment dwell.

* * *

My argument thus far has focused on Shakespeare's sonnets to the young man—admittedly, the bulk of the sequence. But what of the equally famous sonnets to the so-called Dark Lady? At first glance, they would seem to conform roughly to the aesthetic principles I have already described. Sonnet 130, "My mistress' eyes are nothing like the sun," systematically negates the idealizing tropes of Petrarchan poetry, thus producing a desublimated and presumably more "human" mistress—a slightly earthier counterpart to the young man.

Things are not so simple, however. As Jonathan Goldberg has pointed out, "the threatening sexuality that the dark lady represents—outside marriage and promiscuous and dangerous to the homosocial order—is closer to sodomy than almost anything suggested in the sonnets to the young man."[37] To Goldberg's list of sodomitical attributes

I would add that of sterility, conjured most forcefully in Sonnet 129's famous opening line, "Th'expense of spirit in a waste of shame." Among the wealth of possible meanings generated by this line, several turn on the reading of "spirit" as semen and imply a sodomitical waste of the male seed. Like Sonnet 5, then, this one also makes the proper vessel improper by rendering it sterile or nonproductive, and it thereby depicts sex with the Dark Lady as sodomitical in a quite technical sense.

I would argue, moreover, that, just as sodomy is displaced from the young man onto the Dark Lady, so too is the sublime. To make this argument, however, will require reading the Dark Lady sonnets backward, from the perspective of a later writer—one who explicitly employs the category of the sublime and who, moreover, connects it directly with the concept of sodomy. He thus makes open and unmistakable the connections that in Shakespeare are still merely implicit.

The writer I have in mind is the Marquis de Sade, and the book in question is *The 120 Days of Sodom*. I needn't bother recounting much of the plot, since one of the charms of the Sadean novel is that it perfectly conforms to one's preconceptions of it. In brief, however, the book depicts the actions of four debauched libertines who abscond with their young wives, a passel of exquisite, pubescent boys and girls, eight men chosen for the prodigious size of their penises, four middle-aged courtesans expert in the recounting of lascivious tales, four elderly ladies-in-waiting, and three cooks and their assistants. All are confined by the libertines within an impenetrably isolated chateau and (with the exception of the cooks) subjected to an encyclopedic array of tortures and violations.

At the beginning of the novel, where Sade introduces his dramatis personae, he also remarks on the aesthetic principles that will govern his descriptions of them:

> But now let us retrace our steps and do our best to portray one by one each of our four heroes—to describe each not in terms of the beautiful, not in a manner that would seduce or captivate the reader, but simply with the brush strokes of Nature which, despite all her disorder, is often sublime, indeed even when she is at her most depraved. For—and why not say so in passing—if crime lacks the kind of delicacy one finds in virtue, is not the former always more sublime, does it not unfailingly have a character of grandeur and sublimity which surpasses, and will always make it preferable to, the monotonous and lackluster charms of virtue?[38]

If Sade adopts an aesthetics of the sublime for his sodomitical narrative, this is not simply a matter of artistic whim but is, rather, determined by the subjects of his story. The first of his four libertines, the Duc de Blangis, is possessed not only of monstrous and unquenchable appetites, not only of a penis so large that it lacerates and has even been reported to kill its victims, but also of thighs so powerful that they can squeeze the life out of a horse, as he demonstrates to his companions. The Duc de Blangis's body is a source not of beauty but of sexual terror, a titanic and inhuman fount of destructive energies. It is itself sublime. But this bodily aesthetic is not, as one might suppose, reserved only for the male characters of the story. Sade returns to the concept of the sublime when he describes the four elderly ladies-in-waiting, who are chosen in part for their spectacular ugliness. Reflecting on the sexual appeal of such ugliness, he writes:

> Nature's disorder carries with it a kind of sting which operates on the high-keyed sort with perhaps as much and even more force than do her most regular beauties; it has been proven, moreover, that when one's prick is aloft, it is horror, villainy, the appalling, that pleases; ... in the light of all this, there should be no cause for astonishment in the fact that an immense crowd of people prefer to take their pleasure with an aged, ugly, and stinking crone, and will refuse a fresh and pretty girl, no more reason to be astonished at that, I say, than at a man who for his promenades prefers the mountains' arid and rugged terrain to the monotonous pathways of the plains.[39]

Invoking the distinction between mountain and plain, Sade converts a Kantian or Burkean sublime into a sexual aesthetic; and in so doing enables us to extend Lacan's famous articulation of Sade's work and Kant's second critique to include the third critique as well.

The Sadean sublime is exemplified in the portrait of Thérèse, one of the novel's ladies-in-waiting. This portrait is typically Sadean, at once amusingly droll and insanely misogynistic:

> *Thérèse* was sixty-two; she was tall, thin, looked like a skeleton, not a hair was left on her head, not a tooth in her mouth, and from this opening in her body she exhaled an odor capable of flooring any bystander. Her ass was peppered with wounds, and her buttocks were so prodigiously slack one could have furled the skin around a walking stick; the hole in this

splendid ass resembled the crater of a volcano what for width, and for aroma the pit of a privy; in all her life Thérèse declared, she had never once wiped her ass, whence we have proof positive that the shit of her infancy yet clung there. As for her vagina, it was the receptacle of everything ungodly, of every horror, a veritable sepulcher whose fetidity was enough to make you faint away. She had one twisted arm and limped in one leg.[40]

Sade's innovation here is to convert the sublime and beautiful into phys-iological categories. I use "physiology" in its largest sense, since what is involved is not simply appearance—whether bodies strike a beholder as beautiful or ugly—but rather their innermost constitution, which for Sade means the types and quantities of energy that such bodies can gen-erate, conduct, and endure. While the particular portrait examined here happens to be of an aged woman, the division of bodies into beautiful and sublime cuts across differences of age, class, and gender in Sade. President Curval, one of the four male libertines, is, in point of personal hygiene, every bit as appalling as Thérèse.

Despite Sade's earlier evocation of mountains, his sublime descrip-tion of Thérèse is less like a tour of the Alps than like a visit to the Cities of the Plain once God has had his way with them: a landscape at once scarred, bituminous, and mephitic. His anti-blazon, which in its misog-ynist furor recalls Donne's poem "The Comparison," causes the body of Thérèse to recall, indeed literally to incorporate, both the sins of Sodom *and* their divine punishment. Or rather, it evokes these in order to trans-fer this sublime narrative onto Nature. For the atheistical and materialist Sade, sodomy and its punishment are understood not as scenes in a divine comedy but rather as the work of Nature engaging in its one char-acteristic act: that of ceaseless self-destruction. While Shakespeare evokes Nature in Sonnet 20 in order to veil or flee a divine sublimity, Sade invokes Nature in order to usurp it.

Returning to Shakespeare's Dark Lady, we may note that she, like Sade's Thérèse, is the subject of an anti-blazon. And while the Dark Lady's halitosis does not floor bystanders like that of Thérèse, neverthe-less, the poet notes, "in some perfume is their more delight / Than in the breath that from my mistress reeks" (130: 7–8). In contrasting the Lady with perfume, Shakespeare both distances her from the distilling poetics of Sonnet five and establishes an initial point of connection with Thérèse. Indeed, the Dark Lady is a systematic though relatively subdued collection of those attributes that would constitute a Sadean as opposed to a Petrarchan sublime. She is "my female evil" (144: 5), possessed of "so foul a face" (137: 12), and "as black as hell, as dark as night" (147: 14). When he describes her as "the bay where all men ride" (137: 6), Shakespeare not only marks her as sexually insatiable but metaphorically inflates her genitalia to geographical dimensions. In Sonnet 133, the Dark Lady becomes a Sadean torturer, locking both Shakespeare and the young man in her prison. These local parallels, moreover, suggest larger formal and thematic resemblances between the Sadean novel and the Renaissance sonnet sequence. Both are virtuoso attempts at variety within forms that also produce numbing repetition, both denature sexual desire, and both subject the objects of desire to explicit or implicit violence that divides them into fetishized parts.[41]

I have, of course, cited only moments of extreme invective in the Dark Lady series, where Shakespeare also expresses more conventional forms of love and sexual passion. My point, however, is that if Shakespeare's anti-Petrarchan poetics tends at times to humanize the Dark Lady, this should not be seen as a purely desublimating move. Rather, by dismantling the Petrarchan rhetoric of chaste divinity, Shakespeare is laying the groundwork for a counter-sublime. When he displaces the tropes of sodomy from the young man onto the Lady, Shakespeare thereby invests her with a proto-Sadean sublimity, a sublimity that is sodomitical through and through. He thus lays the basis for an aesthetic that will continue through Sade, to Wilde, and beyond.

CHAPTER TWO

Theory to Die For:
Oscar Wilde's *The Portrait of Mr. W.H.*

Toward the end of *The Portrait of Mr. W.H.*, the narrator hears that his friend Erskine has committed suicide, and that he has done so to defend a flawed though fascinating theory of Shakespeare's Sonnets. Horrified by the gratuitousness of this act, the narrator exclaims: "To die for one's theological opinions is the worst use a man can make of his life; but to die for a literary theory! It seemed impossible" (217). Today this is likely to elicit a rueful smile. Knowing as we do how inconsequential literary theory is, we may well feel amused but also wistful in the face of a passion that our discipline cannot (or cannot any longer) generate. To be sure, the profession of literary criticism has created more than its share of martyrs, if we consider professional suicide rather than the mortal kind. Literary theory has helped to lure many a student into graduate careers ending in disappointment and exploitation—blighted lives, though usually not shortened ones.[1] Yet there may be something beyond the unhappy vagaries of the profession—something even more essential—that ties literary theory to martyrdom. Perhaps the pleasures and attractions of theory are allied in part to something like the death drive.

To illustrate: I have recently had occasion to give the first chapter of this book as a talk. And invariably, someone will come up to me afterward and say something like: "But—I thought you were a Marxist!" As I read it, this exclamation enfolds a series of unspoken questions, both sexual and political. One has to do with the (always somewhat murky) nature of my sexual persona, which my choice of subject matter seems to have either clarified or further obscured. And so the first question is: "If you're straight (and are you, by the way?), why are you so interested in sodomy?" The second, more political—but still also sexual—question, is: "If you're a Marxist (and are you, by the way?), why are you so interested in aesthetics—and in sodomy?" Both of my topics offend an institutional understanding of Marxism as an impeccably "manly" school of theory, a view that persists despite considerable evidence to the contrary. In any case, what perplexes my listeners is not only sexual but also theoretical ambiguity. There is apparently something slightly irritating in the fact that my official theoretical "school" does not exhaust my interests—that I am not through and through a Marxist, and nothing but a Marxist, at all times. Despite a recent rhetoric celebrating hybridity of various kinds, this sort of thing is common enough. It bespeaks not only the fiercely identitarian culture of our profession, and a (perhaps innately human) discomfort with cognitive dissonance, but also something about what makes theory alluring in the first place: the dream of a total system that allows for a total identification. Despite their rigor, the abstractions of theory also offer a cocoon in which the self can be happily secreted and dissolved. In a sense, then, what irks my questioners is not so much their puzzlement with me as their disappointment in theory itself, which in this instance has failed to properly digest its practitioner. This is not to say that theory is nothing but an instantiation of the death drive (as if one could dismiss it that way), but simply that this particular pleasure is inseparable from the experience of theory, regardless of what objective intellectual value a particular theoretical school may possess.[2] And, as we have seen often enough, the drive toward self-cancellation through theory is not at all incompatible with the most flagrant forms of self-promotion and self-aggrandizement, however logically inconsistent this may appear. What the grief of Wilde's narrator can point to, then, is the fact that every induction by theory involves a martyrdom. Erskine's suicide (it turns out to be a fake, but it alludes to an earlier, genuine one) merely makes concrete an irreducible aspect of literary theory more generally.

The Portrait of Mr. W.H. concerns a particular theory about a particular literary work. But I do not think I am doing violence to the story by reading it as a parable about theory as such. Both Wilde the artist and Wilde the critic have much to say about what animates our impulse to comment on, and theorize about, works of literary art. The *Portrait* brilliantly illustrates the origin, the propagation, and the fatal effects of literary theory within a dense field of desire. It is only by first tracing the somewhat circuitous paths of this theme, moreover, that we may then arrive at Wilde's original articulations of sodomy and sublimity.

* * *

The Portrait of Mr. W.H. opens in Erskine's library, where he and the
narrator discuss the subject of literary forgeries. Erskine produces from
his cabinet what appears to be an Elizabethan miniature of a fair-haired
young nobleman. Upon closer inspection, the portrait proves to be
that of the "W.H." addressed on the dedication page of Shakespeare's
Sonnets. Erskine identifies the portrait as a forgery commissioned by
Cyril Graham, a deceased friend of his, to prove the latter's theory of the
Sonnets. The narrator, already fascinated by the beautiful portrait, asks
to hear Cyril's theory.

Cyril, we learn, was a beautiful and effeminate young man who in
his student days played the female roles in productions of Shakespeare's
plays. Through a close study of the Sonnets he devises his theory that the
W.H. to whom they are dedicated is one Willie Hughes, a boy actor and
the inspiration for Shakespeare's female characters. Erskine refuses to
endorse the theory fully until external proof can be adduced—some
record that a Willie Hughes existed and performed with Shakespeare's
company. After an exhaustive but futile search, Cyril decides to have the
portrait forged and to tell Erskine that he discovered it in an old trunk
bearing the initials W.H. Initially convinced, Erskine then discovers the
forgery by accident. He confronts Cyril and an argument ensues, after
which Cyril commits suicide to prove his faith in the theory.

Hearing this story, the narrator becomes convinced of the truth of
the theory, despite Erskine's skeptical warnings. He goes off to elaborate
and complete it, and then sends the results to Erskine in a letter. Erskine
is now convinced, but the narrator himself mysteriously ceases to believe
in the theory as soon as he mails off the letter. He tries to talk Erskine out
of the theory but fails. Two years later he receives a letter from Erskine
informing him of the latter's intention to commit suicide in defense of
the theory. Investigating, he discovers that Erskine has indeed died, but
of consumption, not suicide. Heartbroken over the loss of his friend, the
narrator takes the portrait and hangs it in his own library, admitting that
"sometimes, when I look at it, I think there is really a great deal to be said
for the Willie Hughes theory of Shakespeare's Sonnets" (220).

Wilde's novella might well be styled a hermeneutic romance in
which literary analysis, aesthetic enthusiasm, and mutely homoerotic
passion are hopelessly entangled. As even my brief summary suggests,
Cyril Graham's theory circulates in a feverish atmosphere. But the erotics

of theory complicate rather than merely cancel more traditional questions of evidence and logical coherence. As we shall see, both the strengths and the weaknesses of the theory, its teasingly persuasive qualities as well as its ultimate failure to convince, nourish its fascinating power.

Cyril's theory draws on a sensitive if somewhat speculative practice of reading. The name Willie Hughes derives from a supposed pun on "Hews" in Sonnet 20, as well as from the undoubted wordplay on the name "Will" scattered throughout the sequence. From Sonnet 38 and elsewhere comes the idea that Willie Hughes serves as the inspiration for Shakespeare's art—not, however, the art of the Sonnets but rather that of the plays, where Willie Hughes' beauty and personality can embody and complete Shakespeare's dramatic art. One of the virtues of the theory, in Cyril's view, is that it construes Shakespeare's interest in Willie Hughes as artistic rather than sexual, and, as a result, "things that had seemed obscure, or evil, or exaggerated, became clear and rational, and of high artistic import" (161). But of course, this aestheticizing tactic not only fails to cancel erotic desire; it facilitates its communication to and by means of the theory itself.

Erskine at first gives the theory his enthusiastic assent: "Of course I was converted at once, and Willie Hughes became to me as real a person as Shakespeare" (162). Soon, however, doubt sets in. In his later conversation with the narrator, Erskine describes Cyril's theory as "evolved . . . purely from the Sonnets themselves, and depending for its acceptance not so much on demonstrable proof of formal evidence, but on a kind of spiritual and artistic sense, by which alone he claimed could the true meaning of the poems be discerned" (160–61). Erskine urges Cyril not to publish his theory until "some independent evidence" can be found to verify the existence of Willie Hughes, but Cyril merely reacts with impatience to what he terms Erskine's "philistine tone of mind" (162).

This initial disagreement establishes thematics of inner and outer that will structure much of what follows. Not only is Cyril's theory based "purely [on] internal evidence" (157), but it can be accepted and understood only by an inner circle or coterie of those with the requisite spiritual and artistic sensitivities. Cyril's cultural esoterics thus complement his introverted literary formalism. The "philistine" Erskine, by contrast, insists on external evidence and, in the mode of warning against it, is actually the first person to suggest publishing Cyril's theory. The conflict of inner and outer not only plagues Cyril's theory, however; it also finds a place inside it. For the narrator's elaboration of the theory is completely in accord with Cyril's original intent when it holds that

> To the Sonnets Shakespeare was more or less indifferent. He did not wish his fame to rest on them. They were to him his "slight Muse," as he calls them, and intended, as Meres tells us, only for private circulation among a few, a very few friends. Upon the other hand he was extremely conscious of the high artistic value of his plays, and shows a noble self-reliance upon his dramatic genius. (175; cf. 160)

Oddly, Cyril's theory of the Sonnets tends to denigrate the art of the Sonnets themselves. Even more oddly, it does so because the Sonnets share the very esotericism on which his own theory relies. Cyril paradoxically formulates a private theory that extols public art, and it is impossible to say whether his disagreement with Erskine manifests the logical tension in his theory, or whether the theory internalizes and displaces the preexisting differences between Cyril and his good friend. One consequence of the theory, in any case, is that it produces a Shakespeare who resembles the "philistine" Erskine as much as he does the more sensitive Cyril. "Shakespeare was a practical theatrical manager as well as an imaginative poet" (161), remarks Erskine, perhaps somewhat defensively.

The paradoxes that afflict the theory and its object also pertain, of course, to Wilde's novella and *its* cultural context. Kate Chedgzoy aptly remarks that in the *Portrait*, "The *Sonnets* are reconstructed in the image of the homosexual coterie publications with which Wilde was himself involved—magazines such as *The Spirit Lamp* and *The Chameleon*, and the collectively written work of homosexual pornography, *Teleny*."[3] Nevertheless, Wilde chose to publish *The Portrait of Mr. W.H.* not in any of these coterie journals but in the much more public forum of *Blackwood's Edinburgh Magazine*.[4] The division between Cyril and Erskine thus reflects Wilde's own conflicted views about his position within different reading publics. In the end, he makes an Erskine-like decision to publish a Cyril-like theory without any independent supporting evidence. Moreover, the choice of publishing venues for the *Portrait* would come back to haunt Wilde, since this story, even more perhaps than *The Picture of Dorian Grey*, gave rise to public doubt about his sexual orientation. At the trials Wilde would have to answer for the suspicions the *Portrait* created, and he was forced to disavow any knowledge or interest in the conclusions drawn about his work by "brutes and illiterates."[5] Who are these nightmare readers but a concentrated form of the philistinism that just barely taints the sensitive Erskine? Wilde's novella tries to stake out a middle ground between the private art of Shakespeare's Sonnets and the public art of his plays—or rather, it tries to encourage a paradoxical shifting of grounds between them, a tactic that succeeded in art but ultimately failed in the courtroom.

As even this preliminary look reveals, the formal issues of proof, evidence, and coherence that seem to surround Cyril Graham's theory quickly turn into aesthetic and erotic ones. Nothing exemplifies this more fully than the portrait itself, forged by Cyril as phony historical evidence for his theory. Not only is this "proof" yet another fiction, but its primary effect on the beholders is not to satisfy their rational demand for evidence but rather to fascinate and captivate them with its beauty. For the narrator, the painting does not prove the theory; rather, the very desire to hear the theory in the first place follows from his viewing of the portrait, which "had already begun to have a strange fascination for me" (154). Much later, he asks himself: "Had I merely been influenced by the beauty of the forged portrait, charmed by that Shelley-like face into faith and credence? Or, as Erskine had suggested, was it the pathetic tragedy of Cyril Graham's death that had so deeply moved me?" (214). The narrator's use of religious language ("faith and credence") to describe his adherence to the theory is repeated throughout the story. Erskine speaks of being "converted" by the theory, and the narrator uses the term "martyrdom" in the passage quoted at the beginning of this chapter. When he first gives him the portrait to quiet his doubts, Cyril says to Erskine: "The only apostle who did not deserve proof was St Thomas, and St Thomas was the only apostle who got it" (163). The portrait does not act as historical proof, therefore, but as a kind of icon—or idol—which inspires something like religious fervor, though compounded of eros. In Wilde's story, then, the theory is an object not of cognitive assent but of belief; issues of proof and evidence are merely the rational tricking out of a process of sexual and aesthetic fascination.

Reflecting on the way belief in the theory is transmitted, Wilde's narrator explains it as the result of what he calls "influence" and defines as "a transference of personality" (213). As we shall see, Wilde gives a distinctive turn to the concept of transference; but we can begin to understand it by reading the word as meaning more or less the same thing for

Wilde as it does for Freud. Indeed, the transmission of Cyril's theory in the *Portrait* illustrates what John Guillory calls the "transference onto theory" in the work of "master theorists" such as Paul de Man.[6] An exemplary reading of transference in the *Portrait* has already been made, if only implicitly, by William A. Cohen, who shows that the movement of Cyril's theory is always mediated through a letter (in the restricted, epistolary sense), and that the itinerary of the letter corresponds precisely to that described by Jacques Lacan in his seminar on Poe's *Purloined Letter.* Writes Cohen:

> The theory's circuit through the story illustrates its indissoluble unity as epistolary object. . . . The repetition of this topos suggests that belief in the theory is material, exchangeable, and indissoluble: its representational form is precisely a letter. Belief "goes out of one" only to lodge itself (temporarily) in the recipient. Like Lacan's formulation of the purloined letter of Poe's story, the theory passes through and locates the subject, but continues ever on its trajectory.[7]

Cohen's reading makes sense of, among other things, the odd fact that Cyril's theory is believed by only one character at a time, for influence causes loss of belief in the person who exercises it over another. What Cohen does not make explicit, however, is that the movement of the letter in Lacan's reading of Poe allegorizes the dynamics of psychoanalytic transference. I will attempt to clarify this latter aspect in Wilde's tale by describing the field of identifications that the letter's path traverses.

Cyril Graham invents a W.H. in his own "wonderfully handsome" (156) and "effeminate" (155) image, for the forged portrait depicts "a young man of quite extraordinary personal beauty, though evidently somewhat effeminate" (153). By imagining the Sonnets' young man as a cross-dressing actor, moreover, Cyril relives the memory of his own student performances, in which he played Rosaline in *As You Like It.* Since Cyril "put an absurdly high value on personal appearance" (156), his narcissistic identification with Shakespeare's young man is unsurprising. However, the structure of this identification becomes clear only if we distinguish between the Freudian ideal ego [*Idealich*] and the ego-ideal [*Ich-Ideal*], or imaginary and symbolic identifications. As Slavoj Žižek writes, "imaginary identification is identification with the image in which we appear likeable to ourselves, with the image representing 'what we would like to be,' and symbolic identification [is] identification with the very place *from where* we are being observed, *from where* we look at ourselves so that we appear to ourselves likeable, worthy of love."[8] Cyril's identification with W.H. is clearly imaginary; but since such identification is, as Žižek notes, "always identification *on behalf of a certain gaze in the Other*" (156), we must then identify the Other whose viewpoint constitutes the perfection of this ideal ego. For the young man of the Sonnets, it is clearly Shakespeare; for Cyril, it is someone who occupies the Shakespearean position with respect to him, who regards him with a Shakespearean gaze—obviously, Erskine. Describing Cyril's portrayal of Shakespeare's Rosaline, Erskine says: "It was a marvelous performance. You will laugh at me, but I assure you that Cyril Graham was the only perfect Rosaline I have ever seen ... the part might have been written for him" (156). Cyril's identification with the boy-actor in Shakespeare's plays originates, then, in Erskine's appraisal. The theory of the Sonnets reconstitutes the situation of this earlier performance in which Erskine's Shakespearean gaze regards Cyril as the "perfect" Rosaline. Cyril's theory does not analyze the Sonnets, then, so much as it simply repeats them. His theory is a symptom that transfers the Sonnets' own structure of desire onto himself and Erskine—or, alternatively, transfers his relation with Erskine onto the Sonnets.

This being the case, Cyril's forging of the portrait is not really an attempt to provide historical "proof" for his theory. For what he presents to Erskine is essentially a portrait of *himself* in the role of the boy-actor. It is intended not to verify anything but to seduce Erskine back into the position of admiring Shakespearean gaze. When Erskine still resists, Cyril responds by killing himself. This densely meaningful suicide is, among other things, Cyril's attempt to complete his identification with W.H. The deceased Cyril now persists only as textual residue (the theory), as portrait of a beautiful young man, and as a mournful memory. Erskine's eyes fill with tears when he first reveals the portrait to the narrator, just as Shakespeare's sonnets mourn their young man in advance, imagining him as already gone ("Your monument shall be my gentle verse" 81: 9). But if Cyril's status as victim of suicide completes his imaginary identification with W.H., his action as perpetrator extends his symbolic identification with Erskine, construing the latter's refusal to believe in the theory as an act of aggression and then literally enacting it on himself.

Just as Cyril's theory is in some sense a repetition of the Sonnets themselves, so the narrator's induction into the theory simply repeats

Cyril's repetition. When, to Erskine's shock and disapproval, the narrator first declares belief in Cyril's theory, "Erskine got up, and looking at me with half-closed eyes, said, 'Ah! how you remind me of Cyril! He used to say just that sort of thing to me'" (167–68). Here the true line of causality reverses the apparent one. It is not simply the case that the narrator reminds Erskine of Cyril because he believes in the theory. Rather, *the narrator believes in the theory in order that he may remind Erskine of Cyril.* What the narrator desires is to be Erskine's object of desire. Hence he establishes an imaginary identification with Cyril and a symbolic one with Erskine. The latter reveals itself when the narrator leaves Erskine's library:

> As I walked home through St. James's Park, the dawn was just break-ing over London. The swans were lying asleep on the smooth surface of the polished lake, like white feathers fallen upon a mirror of black steel. The gaunt Palace looked purple against the pale green sky, and in the garden of Stafford House the birds were just beginning to sing. I thought of Cyril Graham and my eyes filled with tears.

The narrator's tears for Cyril recall those shed by Erskine when he first reveals the forged portrait. He thus substitutes himself for both mourner and object of mourning.

When the narrator next awakens, he is already fully in the grip of an obsessive wish to prove Cyril's theory. But more, he wishes to expand and perfect it. Thus when he succeeds in making sense of an obscure point in the Sonnets he exclaims: "I struck on the true interpretation, which indeed Cyril Graham himself seemed to have missed" (171). It is not enough for the narrator to be Cyril. He must, as it were, out-Cyril Cyril by completing (and thus overgoing) the latter's theory. The sign and goal of his success will be to convince Erskine where Cyril could not, to carry out the intellectual seduction at which Cyril failed.

The narrator's transference is guided not by the imaginary identifi-cation with Cyril, however, but by the symbolic identification that con-stitutes and sustains it. It the gaze of the Other that structures his desire. We have already seen how the narrator's mourning for Cyril recapitulates Erskine's. But Erskine's viewpoint is, as it was for Cyril, also largely inter-changeable with Shakespeare's. Reading through the Sonnets, the narra-tor exults: "I felt as if I had my hand on Shakespeare's heart, and I was counting each separate throb and pulse of passion" (168). It is less Willie Hughes himself than Shakespeare's erotic response to him that excites the narrator, who identifies more with Shakespeare's desiring gaze than with the object of its desire. When he finally feels he has "completed" Cyril's theory, the narrator also completes this hallucinatory identification with Shakespeare:

> I felt as if I had been initiated into the secret of that passionate friendship. . . . Yes: I had lived it all. I had stood in the round theatre with its open roof and fluttering banners, had seen the stage draped with black for a tragedy, or set with gay garlands for some brighter show.... In the side boxes some masked women were sitting. One of them was waiting with hungry eyes and bitten lip for the drawing back of the curtain. As the trumpet sounded for the third time she leant forward, and I saw her olive skin and raven's-wing hair. I knew her. She had marred for a season the great friendship of my life. Yet their was something about her that fascinated me. (210–11)

If we are tempted to smile at the narrator's total subsumption by the Shakespearean gaze, we might do well to reflect on the ultimate sources of that satisfaction that we still find in Shakespearean criticism today, our own symbolic identifications (however apparently vexed) with the Bard.

Having completed Cyril's theory, the narrator excitedly writes his findings up in a letter and mails it to Erskine. But in the process something surprising happens:

> I put into the latter all my enthusiasm. I put into the letter all my faith.
> No sooner, in fact, had I sent it off than a curious reaction came over me. It seemed that I had given away my capacity for belief in the Willie Hughes theory of the Sonnets, that something had gone out of me, as it were, and that I was perfectly indifferent to the whole project. . . . Perhaps the mere effort to convert anyone to a theory involves some sort of renunciation of the power of credence. (212–13)

The reader is likely to interpret the narrator's disappointment as a kind of cure, a Quixote-like recovery of his senses after his delusional identification with Shakespeare. But it actually complements the delusion, since it involves nothing less than a total identification with Erskine's skeptical gaze. It is not the *attempt* to convert Erskine that costs the narrator his faith. It is, rather, the presentiment—correct, in the event—that he will succeed this time. For once Erskine is seduced by the theory, he no longer occupies the position of the skeptical Other for whom this whole play is staged. Hence the position that Erskine formerly occupied is now free for the narrator himself to purloin. And just as the narrator gains his wish to "become" Erskine, Erskine himself completes the reversal by "becoming" Cyril. For not only does his suicide repeat Cyril's, but, as a faked suicide, it repeats Cyril's attempted forgery as well.

The very possibility of such reversals depends on something that Erskine said when he first rehearsed Cyril's theory for the narrator: "As I don't believe in the theory myself, I am unlikely to convert you to it" (154). But of course he does convince the narrator, which suggests that his unbelief not only fails to stand in the way of this conversion but may somehow be fundamental to it. In Wilde's tale, belief is always delegated to another, passed around as a letter from hand to hand. Or, to put it differently, belief is always staged for, and in behalf of, a nonbelieving Other. Skepticism is thus not the opposite of belief but its necessary pre-condition—what drives the passion of belief to its delusional heights. Surely this is what the narrator means when he says, speaking of martyrdom, that "No man dies for what he knows to be true. Men die for what they want to be true, for what some terror in their hearts tells them is not true" (219). What causes the terror in their hearts but that implacable and unbelieving Other for whom martyrdom is staged? Thus we see the fundamental logic of theory and transference as enacted by Wilde's tale. Theory is a sacrifice of the self in an attempt to seduce the Other.

This "moral" of the story pertains not only to the level on which Cyril's theory circulates; it also finds a place within the theory itself. Meditating on W.H.'s profession as actor, the narrator observes:

> Willie Hughes was one of those—
>> That do not do the thing they most do show,
>> Who, moving others, are themselves as stone.
> He could act love, but could not feel it, could mimic passion without real-
> izing it. (179)

As one who can inspire love in others despite (read: because of) the fact that he cannot feel it himself, Willie Hughes becomes the double of Erskine, who transmits belief in the theory because he does not believe in it himself. Acting may even provide the paradigm for the paradoxical communication of theory in Wilde's story. But if W.H., as actor, provides a reflection of the theory inside the theory itself, Wilde as author provides another mirror outside of it. For the question of how theory is transmitted "inside" the fiction surely offers a model for how (and if) Wilde's tale hopes to communicate belief in Cyril's theory to the reader. Paradoxically, the logic of the story insists that Wilde can convince others of the theory only if he does *not* believe in theory himself—that is, if he is like the actor Willie Hughes or the skeptical Erskine.[9] "All bad poetry springs from genuine feeling," wrote Wilde in "The Critic as Artist" (398). "All bad theory as well," *The Portrait of Mr. W.H.* seems to add.

In locating Cyril's theory within the field of the transference, I have thus far treated it largely as a blank token, a mere random marker that serves as medium of erotic exchange among the characters in Wilde's tale. The status of the theory as *letter* certainly illustrates some crucial aspects of the transference, but to regard it as pure signifier is to ignore those qualitative aspects of the theory that suit it to become an object of fascination. One of the most central of these is the theory's focus on encryption, as William A. Cohen observes:

> Returning to the theory proper, the most urgent question facing us is this: what might it mean for an analysis of Shakespeare's sonnets to focus on proper names encrypted within the poetic structure? It is, first of all, a subject encouraged by the sonnets themselves: "Every word doth almost tell my name, / Showing their birth, and where they did proceed." Such an interpretation understands its object to be a puzzle, a surface on which coded information is inscribed; the information is clearly visible to the knowing reader, yet hidden from the untrained eye. The story's narrator enunciates just this method of reading as he gazes on the portrait of Wille Hughes for the first time: "I see some writing there, but I cannot make it out." (222)

Cohen brilliantly explores the figures for encryption in Wilde's tale, from the old chest purported to have contained Willie Hughes' portrait (a hermeneutic image of the Sonnets themselves) to Cyril's very name, and he deftly relates this to the question of encrypted sexual identities. To his fine analysis I would add only speculation on a possible influence. In 1888, the year before the appearance of *The Portrait of Mr. W.H.*, Ignatius Donnelly published a massive, two-volume tome entitled *The Great Cryptogram: Francis Bacon's Cipher in the So-Called Shakespeare Plays.*[10] A populist politician from Minnesota with an obvious taste for arcana (he also published a book on the lost island of Atlantis), Donnelly was the first of the so-called Baconians to present an argument for authorship by applying Bacon's own idea for a cipher to Shakespeare's works.

The parallels between Donnelly's theory and Cyril Graham's are numerous and intriguing, but here I will mention only the obvious fact that Donnelly reads in search of encoded names, as does Cyril, and indeed converts the whole of Shakespeare's corpus into an enormous, elaborate cryptogram whose purpose is to occult the author's true identity. Donnelly's theory, like Cyril's, produces a Shakespeare who isn't the man the public took him for. After publishing his book, Donnelly launched on a promotional tour of Great Britain, and on April 17, 1888 gave a lecture at Westminster Hall that Wilde attended.[11] Wilde was likely intrigued but unconvinced by Donnelly's system; what he took away from the lecture was probably a vivid sense of how the lure of the encrypted text can foster intellectual obsession.[12]

The fascinating power of Cyril's theory derives not only from its focus on encryption, however, but also from a formal quality of the theory itself: its irreducible, and maddening, incompleteness. More precisely, it is complete and incomplete at once, since it displays an admirable internal coherence (to its adherents, anyway) but always lacks that one piece of external, corroborating evidence on which its validity depends. To Erskine, this lack or hole in the theory is manifest: "I saw the one flaw in the theory" (163). By contrast, when the narrator first hears the theory he declares: "It is complete in every detail. I believe in Willie Hughes" (166). His sense of the theory's completeness, however, proves to be a mirage; it hovers in the middle distance, beckoning but never attainable. For despite his initial profession of faith in the completeness of the theory, the narrator nevertheless feels compelled to elaborate it further. Thus, many pages and much research later, he declares: "I collected all the passages that seemed to corroborate this view, and they produced a strong impression on me, and showed me how complete Cyril Graham's theory really was" (175). Later still, after working out the role of the Dark Lady, he insists once more that "My whole scheme of the Sonnets was now complete, and, by placing those texts that refer to the dark lady in their proper position, I saw the perfect unity and completeness of the whole" (205). By this point, the narrator can insure the completeness of the theory only by reconstructing the very object that the theory was meant to explain. If the theory does not correspond to the Sonnets, the Sonnets must be reordered so that they support the theory. Like Shakespeare's Malvolio when faced with a similarly incomplete text, Wilde's narrator decides that "to crush this a little, it would bow to me."

It hardly needs saying that the flaw, or hole, or lack at the center of Cyril's theory is the very thing that grants it the power to captivate. At a moment of despair, the narrator exclaims: "But the proofs, the links—where were they? I could not find them. It seemed to me that I was always on the brink of absolute verification, but that I could never attain to it" (188–89). Wilde's tale provokes a similar kind of hermeneutic frustration, hinting at sexual secrets that the reader can never really prove.[13] The theory's flaw is, moreover, its formal correlate to the skepticism of Erskine's gaze—a locus of nonbelief that provokes belief. Indeed, it is impossible to say whether the course of the transference in Wilde's tale is determined by these tensions at the heart of the theory or whether the theory simply bears the mark of a transferential process that precedes and structures it. Is the hole at the center of the theory a cause or a mark of the way it is transmitted?

Since the missing piece of evidence is never found, Cyril Graham produces two alternatives in an attempt to plug the hole in his theory: the forged portrait, and his own suicide. The portrait, as we have seen, poses as evidence but really relies on its aesthetic and sexual allure. It is a kind of fantasy object, and indeed recalls the Lacanian function of fantasy as screen for a lack in the Other.[14] When the emptiness of the portrait is revealed, however, Cyril resorts to suicide. As Erskine puts it, "in order to show how firm and flawless his faith in the whole thing was, he was going to offer his life as a sacrifice to the secret of the Sonnets" (166). If the theory remains flawed, at least Cyril's faith in it will be proven flawless. Of course, the narrator later punctures the logic of martyrdom, but it is worth contemplating the complex reasoning behind Cyril's gesture. At one level, it acts as a rebuke to Erskine. It says to him: "You do not, or would not, share with me the sensibility that would make the truth of my theory clear to you. You insisted instead on external corroboration, philistine that you are. Fine, then. I'll become what you crave—pure, dead materiality." At the same time, and in a related way, Cyril's martyrdom is an attempt to take onto himself the sins of the theory. Cyril had already compared himself to Christ with his witticism about St. Thomas. By committing suicide with a revolver, Cyril literalizes and materializes the hole in the theory while incorporating it into himself. In effect, he stigmatizes himself in an attempt to cure the flaw in his theory. But this gesture of martyrdom fails. In the end, Cyril merely redoubles the hole instead of plugging it. Indeed, his death opens a hole or void in the very field of Erskine's being, plunging him into endless mourning. For the narrator, too, elaborating the theory is an act of mourning for Cyril that will always remain incomplete. Just as unbelief is the very vehicle through which belief in the theory is propagated, so the attempt to complete or cover over the flaw in the theory is the very means through which holes multiply. Erskine offers a fascinating image when he warns the narrator: "But for heaven's sake don't waste your time in a foolish attempt to discover a young Elizabethan actor who never existed, and to make a phantom puppet the centre of the great cycle of Shakespeare's Sonnets" (215). The "phantom puppet" is at once the nonexistent Willie Hughes and the no-longer-existent Cyril Graham. Erskine's image of a "great cycle" with a dead or empty center describes not only the Sonnets, of course, but also the theory that repeats them. Indeed, it is an image of theory as such, and it illustrates why those who are drawn to it will never leave it.

*　*　*

This chapter, like Cyril Graham's theory, may seem to have gotten caught up in a circular movement. At least, we are no visibly closer to Wilde's articulation of sodomy and sublimity than we were at the start. Nevertheless, a foundation has been laid in the form of two theses: first, that theory circulates in, and is structured by, the field of the transference. And second, that theory as "object" exerts its transferential fascination by means of an irreparable hole at its center. We have arrived at this point by pursuing a Freudian (and Lacanian) concept of the transference. Yet while it foreshadows Freud's version, Wilde's understanding of transference is more capacious than the psychoanalytic one; it includes the latter, but goes beyond it as well. For Wilde, transference defines not only an intersubjective dynamic but an economy of exchange among separate aesthetic and erotic spheres. In his preface to *The Picture of Dorian Gray*, for example, Wilde defines the critic as "he who can translate into another manner or a new material his impression of beautiful things" (235). "Translation" here is merely another word for transference; the critic filters the expression of personality that is the work of art through his own personality,[15] and thereby both transforms and propagates its effects. Critical translation or transference, then, is another version of the "influence" traced in the *Portrait*. But it also involves a transfer, in the case of the visual or plastic arts, from one medium to another. In the *Portrait*, Shakespeare's sonnets are translated both into critical theory (a new "manner") and into the forged portrait (a new "material"). The movement from text to visual object, moreover, merely inverts Shakespeare's original translation of the young man's physical attractions into the beauties of verse ("If I could write the beauty of your eyes," wishes Sonnet 17, quoted by Wilde's narrator; 174). While Shakespeare's sonnets dwell on the concept of beauty, as I have argued in my first chapter, they also raise the question of what "beauty" can mean, if the same word describes the effect produced by the facial features of a young man and that produced by the language of a sonnet. And this difficult translation may be part of what piques Wilde's interest. In "The Critic as Artist," Gilbert sums up this problem when he states that "the critic reproduces the work that he criticizes in a mode that is never imitative, and part of whose charm may really consist in the rejection of resemblance, and shows us in this way not merely the meaning but also the mystery of Beauty, and, by transforming each art into literature, solves once for all the problem of Art's unity" (371). The mystery of Beauty *is* in large part its capacity for transubstantiation from one medium to another, and particularly, as Gilbert states, from the other arts into literature. Language is the privileged medium that allows the other arts to enter into relations of transference, since it dissolves the supposed particularity of the visual into a more generalized medium of exchange. For Hegel, of course, the movement from image to sign is precisely the mark of the sublime; and Gilbert's exalted reference to the "mystery of Beauty" seems to glance at something similar. Paradoxically, the medium of speech manifests an ungraspable or unspeakable aspect within beauty. Gilbert (who apparently acts as Wilde's mouthpiece) even assigns to the critic the sacerdotal ask of fostering art's mysterious power: the critic, he states, "may seek rather to deepen its [i.e., the work of art's] mystery, to raise round it, and round its maker, that mist of wonder which is dear to both gods and worshippers alike. Ordinary people are 'terribly at ease in Zion'" (372). Gilbert's Judaic reference strays beyond the customary limits of Wilde's Hellenism to invoke a more sublime conception of art. The *Portrait*, as Joel Fineman noted, enacts this (sublime) movement from image to sign as it "narrates the progress from an initially false picture to a concluding false letter."[16] The translation among forms of art made possible by language seems, then, to open up another and potentially more troubling route of transference for Wilde, this one between the beautiful and the sublime.

In the *Portrait*, exchange among different artistic media is supplemented by a second and even more important field of translation between the sexual and the aesthetic. Remarking on the neo-Platonic philosophy of the Renaissance, the narrator states that "There was a kind of transference of the expressions of the physical sphere to a sphere that was spiritual, that was removed from gross bodily appetite, and in which the soul was Lord" (185). Here language—a "transference of ... expressions"—enacts that conversion and purification of eros that psychoanalysis would call sublimation. The narrator's elaboration of Cyril's theory centers largely on a sublimating analysis of the procreation sonnets in which "the marriage that Shakespeare proposes for Willie Hughes is the 'marriage with his Muse'" (172). Because Shakespeare's interest in Willie is purely artistic, Cyril's theory cleanses the sonnets of any homosexual taint: "things that had seemed obscure, or evil, or exaggerated, became clear and rational, and of high artistic import" (161).

But the logic of sublimation is not so clear cut as that. For one thing, by opening up a line of transference from the erotic to the aesthetic, it raises the possibility of movement in the other direction. The narrator explicitly addresses this latter movement, but, significantly, only in the context of Shakespeare's relations with the Dark Lady. According to the narrator, Shakespeare tries to save Willie Hughes from his base entanglement with the Dark Lady by seducing her himself. To this end he "forges false words of love." Yet

> It is never with impunity that one's lips say Love's Litany. Words have their mystical power over the soul, and form can create the feeling from which it should have sprung. Sincerity itself, the ardent, momentary sincerity of the artist, is often the unconscious result of style, and in the case of those rare temperaments that are exquisitely susceptible to the influences of language, the use of certain phrases and modes of expression can stir the very pulse of passion, can send the red blood coursing through the veins, and can transform into a strange sensuous energy what in its origin had been mere aesthetic impulse, and desire of art. (199–200)

Once again language is the medium of transference, this time desublimating aesthetic experience into eros in a way that many of his readers feared Wilde's homoerotically insinuating language in the *Portrait* might do. By positing the origins of sexual desire in "mere aesthetic impulse, and desire of art," Wilde's narrator concocts a genealogy of eros that reverses Freudian sublimation and recalls that of St. Paul in Romans 1— perhaps one of the deep sources for this tale of homosexual passion generated by idolatrous worship of an image.[17]

Even apart from the threat of reversal, Wildean sublimation does what all sublimations do: create a double product. It purifies, but it simultaneously exudes a remainder. It can elevate the sexual to a spiritual or aesthetic plane only by separating out an impure portion, and this portion does not simply vanish. Consider the following passage, in which the narrator ponders the nature of the human soul and mysteries of the Sonnets:

> The soul had a life of its own, and the brain its own sphere of action. There was something within us that knew nothing of extension, and yet, like the philosopher of the Ideal City, was the spectator of all time and of all existence. It had senses that quickened, passions that came to birth, spiritual ecstasies of contemplation, ardors of fiery-colored love. It was we who were unreal, and our conscious life was the least important part of our development. The soul, the secret soul, was the only reality.
>
> How curiously it had all been revealed to me! A book of Sonnets, published nearly three hundred years ago, written by a dead hand and in the honour of a dead youth, had suddenly revealed to me the whole story of my soul's romance. I remembered how once in Egypt I had been present at the opening of a frescoed coffin that had been found in one of the basalt tombs at Thebes. Inside there was a body of a young girl swathed in tight bands of linen, and with a gilt mask over her face. As I stooped down to look at it, I had seen that one of the little withered hands held a scroll of yellow papyrus covered with strange characters. How I wished now that I had had it read to me! It might have told me something about the soul that hid within me, and had its mysteries of passion of which I was kept in ignorance. Strange, that we knew so little about ourselves, and that our most intimate personality was concealed from us! Were we to look in tombs for our real life, and in art for the legend of our days? (211–12)

There is much to marvel over here, from the image of unconscious desire as a hieroglyphic script to the tomb that represents both the encrypted soul and Shakespeare's encrypted sonnets. The sudden intrusion of Egyptian imagery in Wilde's tale will become clearer when I explore

Freud's and Hegel's use of Egyptian motifs in Chapter 3. Here I wish to point out the sublimating separation of fleshly passion into disembodied soul in the first paragraph, and soulless body in the second. This division is then reinscribed onto the Egyptian girl, with her pure gilt mask and withered body beneath. Here the grave acts as repository for human left-overs, the bodily remainder of the departed soul. It is true that the embalmed body of the Egyptian girl is not like those "graves filled with rottennesse" used to describe the remainder of alchemical sublimation. Even death is sweetened here. But the image nevertheless signals Wilde's intention to portray both sublimate and remainder, and to hold them in tension.

In the story itself, the portrait of Willie Hughes offers an emblem of aestheticized, sublimed desire. Its alchemical counterpart as object would thus be not the living Cyril Graham but rather Cyril's body after the suicide—a lifeless, material leftover. The portrait's most fundamental antithesis, however, is not an object at all—it is sodomy, encased in a rhetoric about the unspeakable sin that haunts Shakespeare's love for Willie Hughes. Erskine, for instance, asks: "Who was that young man of Shakespeare's day who, without being of noble birth or even of noble nature, was addressed by him in terms of such passionate adoration that we can but wonder at the strange worship, and are almost afraid to turn the key that unlocks the mystery of the poet's heart?" (160). The narrator, for his part, says "There had been critics, like Hallam, who had regretted that the Sonnets had ever been written, who had seen in them something dangerous, something unlawful even" (186–87), and he admits: "I did not care to pry into the mystery of his [Willie Hughes's] sin or of the sin, if such it was, of the great poet who had so dearly loved him" (177). The very vagueness of language allows this obscure sin to loom larger than any mere naming could. If it suggests on the one hand a kind of social delicacy, it also hints at a region beyond speech altogether, a sublimely unnameable thing. This antithetical pairing of the portrait and the rhetoric of sin clearly foreshadows *The Picture of Dorian Gray*. On one side, a pure and eternally youthful male beauty, and on the other, a sinfulness that beggars representation—unviewable in *Dorian Gray*, unspeakable in *Portrait*. If the *Portrait* contrasts image and sign, as Joel Fineman suggests, it also contrasts image with something foreclosed from language—product and precipitate, respectively, of an alchemical separation. It is here that we may begin to grasp the depth of Wilde's indebtedness to the Sonnets. The *Portrait* not only discourses on the aesthetics of the Sonnets; it also performs that aesthetics.

But to what end? What is the purpose, or at least the effect, of invoking the unspeakable? One thing is certain—Wilde's silence does not try to provide protective cover for "the love that dare not speak its name." That notorious phrase, appropriately enough, comes from a poem by Lord Alfred Douglas, "The Two Loves," that alludes to Shakespeare's Sonnet 144. But Wilde had only contempt for Douglas's line, and the poetics of the *Portrait* directly contradict it.[18] Douglas in effect takes the old tag about sodomy and converts it into a form of victimization. The *act* that Christians *ought* not to say now becomes a *love* that *dare* not speak its own name, thus remaking the sublime terror of sodomy into a plea for the right to speak. Whatever one thinks of this strategy, it is clear that Wilde's *Portrait* does not adopt it. For Wilde's rhetoric works to heighten, not disperse, the sense of a dreadful secret. Wilde opts for vague intimations of unnameable sin instead of either portraying homosexual acts directly (as in *Teleny*) or arguing for tolerance (as does John Addington Symonds, for example). Lawrence Danson provides, I think, a fine sense of Wilde's intentions when he discusses the ferocious reviews generated by *The Picture of Dorian Gray*: "The obvious conclusion—that the unspeakable thing is the usual suspect, sodomy—is not so much wrong as incomplete.... The language [of the reviews] is so savagely, inordinately hostile precisely because the physical fact a reader might find lurking under those splendid folds of implication simply does not add up to the critics' sense of the novel's offense" (132). This is exactly right. But it is important to add that such a reaction originates not only in the reviewers' homophobia but also in Wilde's own choice of narrative and rhetorical strategies, which feed on traditional Christian condemnation of sodomy. In a sense, Wilde's commitment to the sublime in his prose fiction overrides any attempt to make same-sex passion acceptable to a broad public, just as, in his personal style, Wilde chose brilliant and devastating wit over ingratiating tactics. Thus, for a certain kind of reader, Wilde's rhetoric of sublimity will simply revive all the old formulas of condemnation. But the void of silence he creates is so absolute, the walls of secrecy and dread surrounding it so steep, that trying to fill it with any merely finite content, including sodomy, will ultimately disappoint. Wilde does not render sodomy sublime so much as he creates a sublimity that sodomy cannot possibly answer to. Thus his writing might, in

a convoluted way and under very favorable circumstances, manage to
render sodomy ordinary after all.

Wilde's rhetoric of sodomitical silence is to the forged portrait
of Willie Hughes what the sublime is to the beautiful, or what the
remainder of sublimation is to the sublimate—its opposite, but also its
counterpart. For just as the portrait embodies the silence of visual representation, so sodomy occupies a silence that is the beyond of representation. And just as the portrait tries to fill the flaw or hole in Cyril's theory
but fails, so the word "sodomy" tries but fails to fill the void of speech
that surrounds and conjures it. (Sodomy is thus a discursive counterpart
to the (anal) hole in the theory that drove its transference.) And this failure to plug the hole in speech is just fine for Wilde, whose fictions often
seem less concerned with lending voice to homosexual acts or desires
than they do with nurturing a space of the unspeakable, as if Wilde had
already seen through the traps of the "repressive hypothesis" that Michel
Foucault would elaborate almost a century later.

Foucault's name is, of course, unavoidable in contexts such as these.
The History of Sexuality has oriented all recent discussions of Wilde by
locating him at the point where homosexual identity emerges from what
had been merely sodomitical acts. Here I would like to return the favor
by situating Foucault in a Wildean tradition—specifically, in Wilde's
project of nurturing a space for the unspeakable. Both the content of
Foucault's theoretical writings and the dynamics of their transmission
follow a trajectory laid bare by *The Portrait of Mr. W.H.*

Foucault describes *Madness and Civilization* (1961), his first major
work, as the "archeology of that silence" (xi) imposed on madness by the
"Great Confinement."[19] Enlightenment culture, whose institutional arm
is the asylum and whose discursive arm is the tradition of philosophical
rationalism supposedly exemplified by Descartes, surrounds madness
with a cordon of silence not entirely unlike that imposed by an earlier,
theological tradition on sodomy. Foucault's project aims, in part, to
renew the dialogue with madness that marked medieval and early modern culture before being definitively interrupted by the Age of Reason.
But the discourse of madness drives speech to its limit even when it is
not being silenced or banished. As a "sovereign enterprise" (278), madness challenges and arraigns the discourse of Reason, notably in the work
of modern thinkers and artists from Nietzsche and Hölderlin to Artaud
and Van Gogh:

> Artaud's *oeuvre* experiences its own absence in madness, but that experience, the fresh courage of that ordeal, all those words hurled against a fundamental absence of language, all that space of physical suffering and terror which surrounds or rather coincides with the void—that is the work of art itself: the sheer cliff over the abyss of the world's absence. (287)

Madness converts the modern work of art into an act of sovereign *dépense* that ruins language and the world in a sublime fit of destruction. Both its enforced silencing and its status as the speaking of the unspeakable might seem to make madness a kind of discursive analogue to sodomy. The last thing I want to do, however, is to reduce the magisterial accomplishment of *Madness and Civilization* to covert autobiography by construing it as a coded discourse on homosexuality. The point is rather that the categories of silence and the unspeakable *precede* Foucault's later engagement with the history of sexuality and provide a matrix within which the latter assumes its distinctive contours. Foucault's early concern with at once protecting and unleashing a space of the unspeakable (especially against the enforced confessions of psychiatry and psychoanalysis) prepares his critique of the repressive hypothesis. And this theoretical priority of the secret and the unspeakable over sexuality, tied to a poetics of the sublime, is what makes Foucault into a powerful disciple, witting or unwitting, of Wilde.[20]

It would not be difficult to trace the evolution of concepts that eventually leads from *Madness and Civilization* to *The History of Sexuality*. But the fact is that Foucault's categories become sexualized long before the publication of the latter work, and in a more illustrative way, through the famous "debate" with Derrida initiated by the latter's "*Cogito* and the History of Madness" (1964).[21] Derrida's essay is too well known, and its details too distant from my purposes here, to merit an exhaustive summary. Briefly, however, Derrida raises the question whether Foucault's history or archaeology of madness does not constitute an act of Reason rather like the ones that Foucault chronicles, and whether it does not, therefore, enact a new "internment" of madness despite its supposedly oppositional stance. In particular, Derrida questions Foucault's claim that the classical period represents an historically punctual "decision" ending a prior dialogue between reason and madness and confining the latter both actually and philosophically. Foucault's historical claim, Derrida tries to show, tends itself to "confine" a long-standing (indeed, "originary") dissension between reason and madness that can be traced back to ancient Greek culture, and that constitutes historicity itself rather than a mere episode within history. The centerpiece of Derrida's argument is a tour-de-force reading of a passage in the *Meditations* showing that, far from banishing unreason, Descartes establishes a hyperbolical madness at the very heart of philosophical reason.

Even at its most superficial level, "*Cogito* and the History of Madness" inaugurates a homosocial economy in which Derrida tries to confiscate Descartes from Foucault by claiming to be the closer, more intimate reader of the former. In his reply essay, "My Body, This Paper, This Fire" (1972), Foucault will turn the tables by insisting that in fact he, and not Derrida, is the truly "close," attentive, and scholarly interpreter of Descartes. A paradoxical strategy attempts to appropriate Descartes through competitively patient, detailed, and loving readings, thereby rescuing him from the opponent's supposedly hasty and tendentious analyses. Descartes's *Meditations* thus become an object of interpretative rivalry not entirely unlike that which surrounds Shakespeare's Sonnets and the forged portrait in Wilde's tale.

The fascination of theory, moreover, turns in Derrida's essay (as in Wilde's tale) on questions of completeness and incompleteness. But while Wilde's narrator is obsessed with completing Cyril Graham's theory and thus eradicating its fatal flaw, Derrida wants to open up what he considers the premature metaphysical closure of Foucault's arguments. Derrida writes: "Without forgetting, *quite to the contrary*, the audacity of Foucault's act in the *History of Madness*, we must assume that a certain liberation of madness has gotten underway, that psychiatry has opened itself up, however minimally, and that the concept of madness as unreason, if it ever had a unity, has been dislocated. And that a project such as Foucault's can find its historical origin and passageway in the opening produced by this dislocation" (38). Against the "powerful gesture of ... internment" (55) represented by Foucault's book, Derrida insists on the dislocations of reason and madness that will allow "passageways" and "openings" to be maintained—in effect, installing a trap door in the windless enclosure of Foucault's discursive asylum. While in some sense this is a subversive act, and thus a hostile one, Derrida also considers it a friendly gesture. For under Derrida's gaze Foucault himself appears less as a unity than as a "dissension" between audacious and conservative, productively mad and oppressively "reasonable" elements. Derrida's deconstruction can thus be construed (and is by the author) as a way of saving Foucault from himself. Derrida is thus not Foucault's enemy but the advocate of his better half. Thus he can insist at one point that "what I am saying here is strictly Foucauldian" (54). In the course of his reading, Derrida becomes more Foucauldian than Foucault, just as Wilde's narrator out-Cyrils Cyril in elaborating the latter's theory.

Not content with this merely homosocial economy, however, Derrida insists on raising it, if only implicitly, to a homoerotic one. This he does from the very opening of the essay, where he announces that "having formerly had the good fortune to study under Michel Foucault, I retain the consciousness of an admiring and grateful disciple" (31). This consciousness carries its burdens as well, for "the disciple knows that he alone finds himself already challenged by the master's voice within him that precedes his own" (31). Such initial gestures of subordination, sincere enough no doubt, signal Derrida's intellectual embarrassment at critiquing his former teacher. But the master-disciple pairing soon takes on additional meanings. Derrida proceeds to deconstruct Foucault's historical confinement of the "dialogue" between madness and reason to the medieval and early modern periods, and he does so by tracing this dialogue back to Greek philosophy, and particularly to the vexed relations between *logos* and *hubris* in Plato's dialogues. But this philosophical move also delivers us to a homosexual milieu, since the *hubris* that both vexes and supports Socratic reason is largely the homoerotic madness explored in the *Phaedrus* and *Symposium*.[22] By thus invoking the scene of Socratic dialectic, Derrida also retroactively revises his own position as disciple of Foucault, implicitly admitting the role of erotic frenzy in philosophical teaching. In effect, he plays Alcibiades to Foucault's Socrates, both loving and deriding his teacher in a discourse that is at once reasoned and passionately hubristic. The Socratic matrix of Derrida's essay is, moreover, something it shares with *The Portrait of Mr. W.H.*, where philosophical debate between men is similarly structured by a Platonic dialectic of *eros* and *anteros*.[23]

Foucault's response to Derrida, it should be said, largely resists taking up this bait. "My Body, This Paper, This Fire," despite the fleshy suggestiveness of the title, engages in a consistently austere rebuttal of its antagonist.[24] Foucault demonstrates no interest in, or tolerance for, Derrida's oblique experiments in philosophical eros. Which is not to say that his essay manages to extricate itself from the web of transference.

As I have already mentioned, Foucault redoubles Derrida's attempt to appropriate Descartes through a practice of "loving" interpretation. And Foucault does allow himself some mordant jibes at Derrida's soi-disant "discipleship." Reversing Derrida's posture as youthful ephebe, Foucault describes him as the "final glory" of an older system of commentary on Descartes (27). Foucault too invokes a pedagogical scene, but one in which Derrida is very much the tyrannical master, not the disciple. Foucault dismisses Derrida's approach as a "well-determined little pedagogy" that "gives ... to the master's voice the limitless sovereignty which allows it to restate the text indefinitely" (27). This sovereignty is exercised over Derrida's nameless pupils though not over Foucault, who silently rebuffs Derrida's erotic playfulness while absenting himself entirely from the scene of Derridean teaching. Nevertheless, he participates in the same game of at once proclaiming and abjuring mastery.

At this point the "dialogue" falls silent for twenty years, until Derrida revives it in a lecture at the Sainte-Anne Hospital, on the occasion of the thirtieth anniversary of the publication of *Madness and Civilization*. That lecture, expanded and included in Derrida's volume *Resistances of Psychoanalysis* (French edition 1996),[25] takes place after Foucault's untimely death. In a reversal strongly reminiscent of *The Portrait of Mr. W.H.*, the disciple has now become a survivor and his critique an act of mourning. Derrida writes with regret that "the shadow [of this heated debate] ... made us invisible to one another, ... made us not associate with one another for close to ten years" (70). The debate itself is seen in retrospect as "a sort of dramatic chain of events, a compulsive and repeated precipitation" (70), again much like the repetitions, the passionate expostulations and bitter schisms that structure Wilde's tale. It is too late, at this point, to claim discipleship, but Derrida still speaks of his relationship with Foucault in words of love. The essay opens as follows:

> When Elizabeth Roudinesco and René Major did me the honor and kindness of inviting me to a commemoration that would also be a reflection, to one of those genuine tributes where thought is conditioned by fidelity and fidelity honed by thought, I did not hesitate for one moment.
>
> Above all, because I love memory. This is nothing original, of course, and yet, how else can one love? Indeed, thirty years ago this great book of Foucault was an event whose repercussions were so intense and so multiple that I will not even try to identify, much less to measure them, deep

inside me. [*Or, ce grand livre de Foucault fut il y a trente ans un événement dont je ne tente même pas d'identifier, encore moins de mésurer au fond de moi, le retentissement tant il fut intense et multiple dans ses figures.*][26]

At the risk of violating decorum, I cannot resist pointing out the sexual overtones of "those repercussions ... so intense and multiple that I will not even try to identify, much less measure, them deep inside me." The original French is even more suggestive, since the phrase *au fond de moi*, "deep inside me" or "at my very core," also hints at the more literal sense of *fond*, thus suggesting something like "at my bottom" or "at my fundament." In commemorating the publication of Foucault's book, Derrida seems also to be revisiting the scene of his Socratic discipleship to Foucault, and I think it is no exaggeration to suggest that these sublimely unmeasurable and shattering repercussions are the aftershocks of theoretical sodomy, or rather, of an imaginary act of sodomy *by means of* theory. Not only does this moment render concrete Derrida's habitual theoretical posture (he is nothing if not a pushy bottom), but it also captures several elements of a Wildean rhetoric, notably a recourse to tropes of the sublime combined with teasingly powerful but unverifiable suggestions of sexual transgression.

Foucault's *Madness and Civilization* is thus sexualized through its transference both long before and after the publication of *The History of Sexuality*. That transference unfolds, moreover, along strictly Wildean lines. The triangulations of Descartes, Foucault, and Derrida reproduce those of Cyril Graham, Erskine, and the narrator in Wilde's tale. In both fact and fiction, the homosocial transmission of theory not only takes on a sodomitical cast but brushes up against a poetics of the sublime. The Derrida-Foucault debate does, however, throw light on an aspect of theory that I neglected in my reading of Wilde. Derrida's commemorative essay on Foucault is, as I have said, an act of mourning. But not of mourning in the Freudian sense, in which the bereaved subject works through the loss of the object in order finally to have done with it. Derrida rather engages in what would have to be called a kind of posthumous dialogue with Foucault, an attempt to keep a conversation going despite the loss of his enemy-friend.[27] In this regard, Derrida's insistence on reopening what he regards as prematurely closed in Foucault, on cutting a trap door into the asylum, is also an effort to keep Foucauldian theory perpetually open to the future—in effect, to maintain it as a living/dead body—a project not unlike that undertaken proleptically by Shakespeare with regard to his young man, or by Wilde's narrator in relation to Cyril. If theory is to die for, source of a pleasure allied with the death drive, it can also be a source of reanimation. For Derrida (as for Wilde's narrator), the lost beloved still lives, if only in theory.

CHAPTER THREE

Freud's Egyptian Renaissance: *Leonardo da Vinci and a Memory of His Childhood*

Freud begins his famous study of Leonardo da Vinci in a stance of mock-defensiveness, assuring his readers that he intends no blasphemy:[1]

> When psychiatric research, normally content to draw on frailer men for its material, approaches one who is among the greatest of the human race, it is not doing so for the reasons so frequently ascribed to it by laymen. "To blacken the radiant and drag the sublime into the dust" [*das Strahlende zu schwärzen und das Erhabene in den Staub zu ziehn*] is no part of its purpose, and there is no satisfaction for it in narrowing the gulf which separates the perfection of the great from the inadequacy of the objects that are its usual concern. (*S.E.* 11: 63; *G.W.* 8: 128)[2]

In some respects, at least, Freud has every intention of narrowing the gulf between Leonardo and the rest of us. He merely denies that cultural iconoclasm gives him pleasure or satisfaction, though his denial must itself create doubts. In any case, the idol to be smashed is not Leonardo himself but the falsified image of him created by censoring biographers—"a cold, strange, ideal figure, instead of a human being to whom we might feel ourselves distantly related" (130).[3] Only thus, claims Freud, can the sublimity of Leonardo's art be properly understood and exalted.

Freud's ambivalent worship of Leonardo is nowhere more apparent than in his treatment of the artist's homosexuality. To focus on this issue, and on Leonardo's infantile sexual life, is primarily what Freud has in mind when he writes of "blackening the radiant." And yet Leonardo's homosexuality, as Freud constructs it, is itself "ideal" (*ideel*) or sublimated. Leonardo was both charged with sodomy and acquitted of the charge (71–72), a fact that fits perfectly into Freud's view of him as a man whose sexual drives were diverted entirely to artistic creation and scientific research (19).[4] "Leonardo," he writes, "represented the cool repudiation of sexuality," and in his "frigidity" (*Frigidität*, 69; *G.W.* 8: 136), he comes to resemble the "cold, strange, ideal figure" that Freud otherwise claims to be dismantling. For Leonardo, to be homosexual is to approximate the condition of statuary. Leonardo's petrification serves at least two purposes. Detaching homosexuality from sodomy makes it into an interior, subjective state—in short, a (pathological) identity. "What decides whether we describe someone as homosexual is not his actual behavior," writes Freud, "but his emotional attitude" (87).[5] For psychoanalysis, the chaste Leonardo is thus a purer embodiment of "the homosexual" than any practicing sodomite could ever be. Moreover, as Freud claims in his essay "'Civilized' Sexual Morality," "The constitution of people suffering from inversion—the homosexuals—is, indeed, often distinguished by their sexual instinct's possessing a special aptitude for cultural sublimation" (*S.E.* 9:190). Leonardo is not merely a sublimated homosexual, then, but a spectacular example of homosexuality's supposed drive to sublimate itself. If homosexuality turns spontaneously to art, it is no wonder that Leonardo himself crystallizes into a kind of statue.

All this talk of idolatry, statues, and iconoclasm would suggest that Freud's conversion of the premodern sodomite into the modern homosexual does not simply abandon the older set of cultural associations surrounding the former. Nor is it mere chance that his book on Leonardo opens with a reference to the sublime—more specifically, to the idea of debasing or ruining the sublime. As we shall see, the Egyptian motifs running throughout the Leonardo book both invoke Hebraic sublimity and point to its regressive undoing in Leonardo's life and art. Moreover, the book's implicit cultural narrative is interwoven with the oedipal narrative underlying Leonardo's sexuality. Freud's Egypt is the land not only of the pharaohs but also of the male homosexual, in particular the male homosexual as artist. And, not incidentally, it is central to Freud's radical recasting of Renaissance culture.

*   *   *

Freud's study of Leonardo is his most extended effort to probe the mysteries of sublimation. Analyzing his infantile fantasies and conflicts, Freud claims both to trace the origins of Leonardo's homosexuality and to show how his sexual drives were diverted to artistic and scientific activities. In drawing a portrait of the sublimating-homosexual-as-artist, Freud continues a line that runs from Plato to Oscar Wilde. While he comes to praise Leonardo, however, Freud also remakes him into the stereotype of the maternally dominated male homosexual and contemptuously dismisses the views of those who contest the psychoanalytic construction of homosexuality.

What makes the Leonardo book into either an interpretive tour de force or rampant fantasy is the scantiness of matter on which Freud is forced to build his case. Much of Freud's inspiration comes not from historical annals at all but from a novel about Leonardo's life by the Russian writer D. S. Merezhkovsky. Some basic facts are beyond dispute: Leonardo was born in 1452, the illegitimate son of Ser Piero da Vinci, a notary, and a woman named Caterina. Beyond that, "the only definite piece of information about Leonardo's childhood," writes Freud, "comes in an official document of the year 1457; it is a Florentine land-register for the purposes of taxation, which mentions Leonardo among the members of the Vinci family as the five-year-old illegitimate child of Ser Piero" (81). But there is one additional piece of information, from the pen of Leonardo himself. In one of the entries in his voluminous notebooks, Leonardo records a childhood memory: "It seems that I was always destined to be so deeply concerned with vultures; for I recall as one of my very earliest memories that while I was in my cradle a vulture came down to me, and opened my mouth with its tail, and struck me many times with its tail against my lips" (82). What I have just quoted is an English translation not of Leonardo's Italian but of Freud's notoriously inaccurate German translation, which substitutes "vulture" for the Italian *nibbio* or "kite." This error was portentous both for the direction of Freud's reading and for the future reception of his book, which has been dissected by critics on historical and art-historical grounds.[6]

Freud's reading of the "vulture" scene begins predictably: the tail is a phallic symbol (the Italian *coda* also being slang for "penis"), and thus the memory is really a phantasy of fellatio. But that phantasy in turn leads back to an older memory of sucking at the mother's breast (86–87). Condensing these elements, the memory "indicate[s] the existence of a causal relation between Leonardo's relation with his mother in childhood and his later manifest, if ideal homosexuality" (98). Freud develops this narrative of origins through what he admits is a tendentious reading of the document listing Leonardo as a member of his father's household at age five. Assuming that Leonardo lived alone with his mother until roughly this age (an assumption that documentary evidence has since definitively disproven), Freud installs the infant Leonardo in a kind of pre-oedipal utopia allowing unchallenged access to the mother. This early period of isolation with Caterina is fateful in several ways. By allowing the young Leonardo to indulge both his early sexual researches and his scopophilic instincts without restraint, it channels his sexual drives along lines that would later reinforce his scientific and artistic pursuits, thus predetermining the paths of his sublimations, which would begin at puberty (132). The effects on his sexual identity are no less profound. As Freud points out, the absence of a father deprives the male child of the identification necessary to produce a heterosexual object choice, and thus his pre-oedipal idyll soon takes a mysterious turn:

> After this preliminary stage a transformation sets in whose mechanism is known to us but whose motive forces we do not yet understand. The child's love for his mother cannot continue to develop consciously any further; it succumbs to repression. The boy represses his love for his mother: he puts himself in her place, identifies himself with her, and takes his own person as a model in whose likeness he chooses the new objects of his love. In this way he has become a homosexual. What he has in fact done is to slip back to auto-erotism: for the boys whom he now loves as he grows up are after all only substitutive figures and revivals of himself in childhood—boys whom he loves in the way in which his mother loved *him* when he was a child. He finds the objects of his love along the path of *narcissism*, as we say; for Narcissus, according to the Greek legend, was a youth who preferred his own reflection to everything else and who was transformed into the lovely flower of that name.
>
> Psychological considerations of a deeper kind justify the assertion that a man who has become a homosexual in this way remains unconsciously fixated to the mnemic image of his mother. By repressing his love for his mother he preserves it in his unconscious and from now on remains faithful to her. While he seems to pursue boys and to be their lover, he is in reality running away from the other women, who might cause him to be unfaithful. (99–100)

Recalling the Lacanian model I employed in my chapter on Wilde, we may say that the male homosexual establishes an imaginary identification with his younger self (that is, he takes his younger self as his idealized object of desire) and a symbolic identification with his mother (since it is from her perspective that his younger self is ideal).

Elevating the mother to ego-ideal, moreover, implants the seed for a maternal superego, as I shall detail below. First, however, another element of Freud's analysis deserves mention. Freud claims that "a man who has become homosexual ... remains fixated to the mnemic image of his mother. By repressing his love for his mother he preserves [*konserviert*] it in his unconscious and from now on remains faithful to her." Not only does this double process of repression and conservation have a vaguely Hegelian cast, but it results in a kind of encrypting of the maternal image, both burying it and preserving it intact. In fact, Leonardo will memorialize his mother in a way that literalizes and repeats this earlier psychic encryption.[7] As Freud points out, Leonardo's notebooks contain almost no reference to his parents or expression of his emotional attachment to them. They do, however, contain records of certain household expenses, including a florin-by-florin account of the costs for the funeral of a woman named Caterina. Freud accepts Merezhkovsky's belief that this Caterina was Leonardo's mother rather than a servant girl of the same name, and concludes that "What we have before us in the account of the costs of the funeral is the expression—distorted out of all recognition—of his mourning for his mother" (105). What Freud says of Leonardo's notebook entry holds for Leonardo's homosexuality as well, which Freud likewise sees as a distorted form of mourning for the encrypted mother. I shall elaborate on the aesthetics of encryption in this chapter's third section.

In Leonardo's case, maternal identification rules both his personal life and his art. While Freud denies that Leonardo ever engaged in sexual relations with men, he notes that the artist chose "only strikingly handsome boys and youths as pupils. He treated them with kindness and consideration, looked after them, and when they were ill nursed them himself, just as a mother nurses her children and just as his own mother might have tended him" (102). Freud also quotes with satisfaction Vasari's testimony that "In his youth [Leonardo] made some heads of laughing women out of clay, which were reproduced in plaster, and some children's heads which were as beautiful as if they had been modelled by the hand of a master." Freud adds: "Thus we learn that he began his artistic career by portraying two kinds of objects; and these cannot fail to remind us of the two kinds of sexual objects [i.e., mother and male child] that we have inferred from the analysis of his vulture phantasy" (111).

Freud's analytical powers are brought to bear in a more sustained way upon two of Leonardo's masterpieces: the *Mona Lisa* and the painting known in German as the *Heilige Anna Selbdritt* or *St. Anne with Two Others*. In the latter painting the Virgin Mary sits on the lap of her mother, St. Anne, and reaches toward the Christ child, who plays with a lamb in the lower right-hand corner. Freud reads this painting as an overdetermined reworking of Leonardo's pre-oedipal idyll. The two mother figures can be read as Leonardo's natural mother Caterina and Donna Albiera, the stepmother into whose care he was placed when he moved to his father's household, or, alternatively, as Donna Albiera and Leonardo's paternal grandmother, who also lived with her son and his wife (112–13). Freud emphasizes the way in which Leonardo's painting—and even more so an earlier drawing of the theme—makes it difficult to separate the figures of St. Anne and the Virgin, who are "fused with each other like badly condensed dream figures" (114, n. 1). This merging of maternal bodies signals not only the similarity in Leonardo's own mind of his various female caretakers but also, one assumes, the indistinct boundaries between self and (m)other in the pre-oedipal union. The absence of father-figures and the "blissful smile of the joy of mother-hood" (113) with which both Anne and Mary are endowed merely completes the happiness of Leonardo's infantile pastoral, though things are more complex than this first brief summary would suggest.[8]

In any case, Freud views the *Heilige Anna Selbdritt* as an expansion and reworking of themes already broached in the *Mona Lisa*. The latter, however, portrays motherhood in a far more ambivalent guise. Freud cites a number of authorities, including Walter Pater, who find something sinister in the fascinating enigma of Mona Lisa's smile, and he summarizes by stating that her expression offers "the most perfect representation of the contrasts which dominate the erotic life of women; the contrast between reserve and seduction, and between the most devoted tenderness and a sensuality that is ruthlessly demanding—consuming men as if they were alien beings" (108). Moreover, he concludes that the smile of Mona Lisa del Giocondo, the model for the painting, reawakened in Leonardo a memory of his own mother's smile, which henceforth became the model for the unmistakable Leonardesque smile in the *St. Anne, Leda, St. John*, and *Bacchus* (110–11, 117).

The sinister elements in Mona Lisa's smile cast a shadow on Leonardo's early relations with his mother. Freud elucidates these elements by returning to the vulture fantasy:

In words which only too plainly recall a description of a sexual act ("and struck me many times with its tail against my lips"), Leonardo stresses the intensity of the erotic relations between mother and child. From this linking of his mother's (the vulture's) activity with the prominence of the mouth zone it is not difficult to guess that a second memory is contained in the phantasy. This may be translated: "My mother pressed innumerable kisses on my mouth." The phantasy is compounded from the memory of being suckled and being kissed by his mother. (107)

But while these kisses complete Leonardo's pre-oedipal idyll, they also threaten to overwhelm the young boy:

The violence of the caresses, to which his phantasy of the vulture points, was only too natural. In her love for her child the poor forsaken mother had to give vent to all her memories of the caresses she had enjoyed as well as her longing for new ones; and she was forced to do so not only to compensate herself for having no husband, but also to compensate her child for having no father to fondle him. So, like all unsatisfied mothers, she took her little son in place of her husband, and by the too early maturation of his erotism robbed him of a part of his masculinity. (115–17)

Ironically, despite the absence of a threatening father, the consummation of pre-oedipal love produces something like castration, at once prematurely awakening Leonardo's masculinity and "robbing" him of it. The violent intensity of maternal demand takes the place of the father's castration threats, and has, if anything, a more deeply traumatic effect.[9] Leonardo's identification with his mother has at its basis this traumatic core, which gives rise to a kind of maternal superego, endlessly issuing not the paternal "No" but an equally insistent, tyrannical, and unfulfillable demand for enjoyment. In the course of his Leonardo book Freud twice invokes *Hamlet* (121, 137), perhaps seeing in Hamlet and Gertrude a literary parallel to the problems that maternal demand poses for Leonardo.

But if the maternal superego at once creates and suspends Leonardo's homosexuality, its effect on his art is less equivocal. For what imposes paralysis in the sexual sphere also produces the endlessly fascinating and enigmatic smile of the *Mona Lisa*. Freud's analysis of this painting deserves further study, because it reveals the radically innovative nature of his, and Leonardo's, aesthetics. The crucial factor in Freud's reading (though he cites precedent for this move) is the displacement of aesthetic focus downward from the eye to the mouth. What fascinates in the Mona Lisa is not her gaze but that smile which is at once tender and devouring. We can gauge the importance of this displacement downward by comparing Hegel's treatment of physiognomy in his discussion of Greek statuary art. "In the formation of the animal head," argues Hegel, "the predominant thing is the mouth, as the tool for chewing, the upper and lower jaw, the teeth, and the masticatory muscles. The other organs are added to this principal organ only as servants and helpers: the nose especially as sniffing out food, the eye, less important, for spying it. The express prominence of these formations exclusively devoted to natural needs gives the animal head the appearance of being merely adapted to animal functions and without any spiritual or ideal significance." By contrast, writes Hegel,

> if the human appearance in its bodily form is to bear an impress of the spirit, then those organs which appear as the most important in the animal must be in the background in man and give place to those indicative not of a practical relation to things but of an ideal or theoretical one.
>
> Therefore the human face has a second centre in which the soulful and spiritual relation to things is manifested. This is the upper part of the face, in the intellectual brow, and, lying under it, the eye, expressive of the soul, and what surrounds it. That is to say that with the brow there are connected meditation, reflection, the spirit's reversion into itself while its inner life peeps out from the eye and is concentrated there. (2: 729)[10]

The eye is the organ of the theoretical and spiritual sense, while the mouth embodies practical, animal need. Hence the Greek profile, which Hegel extols, emphasizes those upper regions of the face and head that signify not only the spirituality of the depicted figure but also (presumably) that of the viewer, whose own gaze becomes meditative and non-appetitive in the presence of art. By negating the mouth, and therefore practical need, the eye sustains the ideality of art itself as Hegel understands it.

Freud's reading of the *Mona Lisa* can be understood, then, as systematically inverting the values of German idealist aesthetics. By relocating the center of the painting from eye to mouth, Freud abandons the realm of intellect or spirit for that of the oral drives. The language used to describe Mona Lisa's sensuality—"consuming men as if they were alien beings" (*den Mann wie etwas Fremdes verzehrenden*, 108; *G.W.* 8:

179–80)—recalls Hegel's association of the mouth and animal feeding, but in this case the hunger is sexual. The mouth, moreover, does not simply replace the eye here; in a sense, it negates it. For Mona Lisa's smile greets the viewers gaze not with a countergaze but with a ravening need that does not see its object except to consume it. Hers is precisely a Miltonic "blind mouth," the empty stare of traumatically insistent demand.

Freud's "displacement downward" from eye to mouth might seem to shift the *Mona Lisa* below the threshold of the beautiful. Yet Freud hopes to explain, not negate, the painting's aesthetic power. In his analysis the Mona Lisa is undeniably beautiful, but at the same time she threatens to consume or annihilate the viewer, reversing the normal situation in which the viewer aesthetically "consumes" the artwork. Hence the painting's traumatically fascinating image is an unconventional instance of the sublime. Indeed, it can be said to inaugurate a specifically *maternal sublime*, and this is its fundamental aesthetic innovation. Just as Freud transforms sodomy (a transgression of divine law) into homosexuality by replacing the paternal with a maternal superego, so he reconfigures the categories of classical aesthetics by "maternalizing" the traditionally masculine category of the sublime.[11] He thereby preserves the longstanding link between sodomy and sublimity even while warping each of the two terms almost beyond recognition.

These older connections come quite close to the surface in Freud's discussion of the *Bacchus* and *John the Baptist*, two late works in which androgynous male figures wear the famous Leonardesque smile. "These pictures," writes Freud, "breathe a mystical air into whose secret one dares not penetrate. . . . They are beautiful youths of feminine delicacy and with effeminate forms; they do not cast their eyes down, but gaze in mysterious triumph, as if they knew of a great achievement of happiness, about which silence must be kept" (117). In almost Wildean tones, Freud describes paintings that impart the silence of an unspeakable secret. Like the picture of Dorian Gray or the portrait of Mr. W.H., Leonardo's late paintings enfold a transgressive dream. In this case, however, the dream is not sodomitical but pre-oedipal, "representing the wishes of the boy, infatuated with his mother, as fulfilled in this blissful union of male and female natures" (118). For Leonardo, in any case, homosexuality is merely the echoing symptom of this original desire. While sodomy invokes the sublime fear of the punishing father, Leonardo's homosexuality invokes the equally annihilating wish for pre-oedipal union with the mother. The

Leonardesque sublime arises from a vertiginous proximity to the maternal Thing, the subject of out next and final chapter.

*   *   *

Freud's rendering of *nibbio* or kite as "vulture" may be his most famous blunder. Since first pointed out in 1923, it has certainly made it easy for critics to dismiss his study of Leonardo.[12] The error would not be so serious if it did not lead Freud into a long and detailed excursus on the place of vultures in Egyptian mythology, which then forms one of the principal supports for his analysis of Leonardo's phantasy. "In the hieroglyphics of the ancient Egyptians," Freud informs us, "the mother is represented by a picture of a vulture. The Egyptians also worshipped a Mother Goddess, who was represented as having a vulture's head, or else several heads, of which one was a vulture's" (88). Moreover, ancient lore held that only female vultures existed, and that, to reproduce, they would "pause in mid-flight, open their vagina," and be "impregnated by the wind" (89). The Fathers of the Church frequently invoked this myth to support the doctrine of the Virgin Birth, which is how, Freud surmises, Leonardo learned of it. This bit of erudition was then retroactively intermixed with Leonardo's childhood memories to form the "vulture" phantasy, where it signified "that he had also been such a vulture-child— he had a mother, but no father" (90). In addition, "this vulture-headed mother goddess was usually represented by the Egyptians with a phallus; her body was female, as the breasts indicated, but it also had a male organ in a state of erection" (94). The vulture represents the phallic (pre-oedipal) mother and also helps connect the fellatio and nursing phantasies that are integrated in Leonardo's childhood "memory." (It also, incidentally, recalls the "master-mistress" of Shakespeare's Sonnet 20.) Egyptian vulture-lore is thus crucial to Freud's construction of the memory as bearing on Leonardo's pre-oedipal relations with his mother and his eventual homosexuality.

Of course there is no vulture in Leonardo's childhood memory, which causes this elegant edifice to come crashing down.[13] But the question then is why Freud makes the error in the first place. The fact that he relied on a faulty German translation of the notebooks provides a partial but not a full explanation, since he also had access to the Italian text, and his Italian was good enough to have caught the mistake. Thus psychoanalytic readers have been tempted to find a deeper logic behind this Freudian slip, a temptation that is strengthened by Freud's all-too-obvious identification with Leonardo.[14] The most compelling context for understanding Freud's Egyptian excursion comes from one of the auto-biographical dreams analyzed in *The Interpretation of Dreams*, in the section of chapter 7 on anxiety dreams.[15] I shall quote the dream and Freud's analysis in full, since it has a powerful bearing on my own argument.

It is dozens of years since I myself had a true anxiety-dream. But I remember one from my seventh or eighth year, which I submitted to interpretation some thirty years later. It was a very vivid one, and in it I saw *my beloved mother, with a particularly peaceful, sleeping expression on her features, being carried into the room by two (or three) people with birds' beaks and laid upon the bed.* I awoke in tears and screaming, and interrupted my parents' sleep. The strangely draped and unnaturally tall figures with birds' beaks were derived from the illustrations to Philippson's Bible. I fancy they must have been gods with falcons' heads from an ancient Egyptian funerary relief. Besides this, the analysis brought to mind an ill-mannered boy, a son of a *concierge*, who used to play with us on the grass in front of the house when we were children, and who I am inclined to think was called Philipp. It seems to me that it was from this boy that I first heard the vulgar term for sexual intercourse, instead of which educated people always use a latin word, "to copulate," and which was clearly enough indicated by the choice of the falcons' heads. I must have guessed the sexual significance of the word from the face of my young instructor, who was well acquainted with the facts of life. The expression on my mother's features in the dream was copied from the view I had had of my grandfather a few days before his death as he lay snoring in a coma. The interpretation carried out in the dream by the "secondary revision" must therefore have been that my mother was dying; the funerary relief fitted in with this. I awoke in anxiety, which did not cease till I had woken my parents up. I remember that I suddenly grew calm when I saw my mother's face, as though I had needed to be reassured that she was not dead. But this "secondary" interpretation of the dream had already been made under the influence of the anxiety which had developed. I was not anxious because I had dreamt that my mother was dying; but I interpreted the dream in that sense in my preconscious revision of it because I was already under the influence of the anxiety. The anxiety can be traced back, when repression is taken into account, to an obscure and evidently sexual craving that had found appropriate expression in the visual content of the dream. (*S.E.* 5: 583–84)

Freud's interest in Egyptian bird-figures thus dates from his childhood, where it is associated (as in the Leonardo book) with the figure of the mother. The connection between birds and sexuality is implied by the dirty word that the concierge's son teaches young Sigmund: *vögeln*, which means "to fuck" but also, literally, "to bird." (Freud invokes this word in the Leonardo study as well; 125.) Freud remains pointedly vague about the forbidden wish that generates the anxiety in his dream, describing it only as "an obscure and evidently sexual craving," though it clearly has something to do with the sleeping/dead mother. Significantly, this craving remains unattached to any grammatical subject.[16] One naturally assumes that it is Sigmund's, but it could also be the mother's, whose "peaceful, sleeping expression" suggests postcoital satiety. We therefore seem to be in a realm not unlike that of Leonardo's pre-oedipal idyll, where desire for the mother is met (and overmatched by) the desire of the mother. By breaking into his parents' bedroom, the young Sigmund convinces himself that his mother is still alive, but also (and this is really the same thing), that she is not the subject of an overpowering sexual enjoyment.

The bearer of the "sexual craving" is rendered even more ambiguous by the interplay of facial expressions in the dream. In his analysis, Freud notes that "I must have guessed the sexual significance of the word [*vögeln*] from the face of my young instructor," and then immediately goes on to discuss "the expression on my mother's features in the dream." So contiguity alone suggests some connection between the lewd expression of triumph on Philipp's face and the peaceful expression on his mother's. The "ill-mannered" concierge's son clearly takes pleasure in shocking Sigmund and also in imparting a piece of sexual—and sexualized—knowledge. In effect, he "birds" Freud by teaching him the word for "birding."[17] Several strands of the Leonardo study thus converge here: the connection between knowledge and sexual investigation, the traumatic initiation into sexuality, and, no less important, a transitive interplay between the mother's sexuality and that of a young man. Finally, there is the connection between Egyptian art and the encryption of the mother. The bird-headed figures who bear Freud's mother on a bed are taken from "an ancient Egyptian funerary relief," which suggests that this dream is not only about fears of the mother's actual demise but also about the very process by which the traumatizing mother is "encrypted" (buried but preserved) in the unconscious. Freud's identification with Leonardo is, then, very deep indeed.

My interest in Freud's childhood dream, however, focuses on the points of contact between these "psychological" themes and more cultural ones involving Freud's Jewishness. Pursuing these will allow us to refine and deepen our understanding of how Freud constructs a "sublime" homosexuality. The images of bird-headed figures, Freud tells us, come from "Philippson's Bible." *Die Israelitische Bibel*, an edition of the Hebrew scriptures with facing German translation, was the Freud family bible. Edited by Ludwig Philippson, it contained ample scholarly commentary accompanied by numerous woodcuts, many from Egyptian sources. Freud's family owned the second edition (1858), and it would not be at all surprising to find that a young child like Sigmund was drawn more to the exotic woodcuts than to the often forbidding text. The Philippson bible contains more than one illustration of bird-headed Egyptian gods as well as birds in funerary contexts.[18] One of these, mentioned by James Strachey in a note to the Standard Edition, appears in Philippson's commentary on chapter four of Deuteronomy (see Figure 1).

The Philippson bible was thus a familiar household object of Freud's childhood, but it was destined to return (much like the repressed) in his adult life. In 1891, for Freud's thirty-fifth birthday, his father Jacob had the old family bible (or at least the second of three volumes) bound in leather and presented it to his son as a gift. To accompany the bible, Jacob composed an elaborate inscription in Hebrew. Yosef Hayim Yerushalmi notes that the inscription "is written entirely in *melitzah*, a mosaic of fragments and phrases from the Hebrew Bible as well as from rabbinic

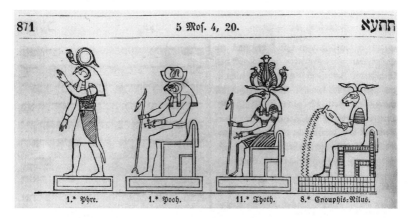

Figure 1. Ludwig Phillipson, *Die Israelitische Bibel* (Leipzig: Baumgärtners Buchhandlung, 1844–54). Dorat Jewish Division, The New York Public Library, Lenox and Tilden Foundations.

literature or the liturgy, fitted together to form a new statement of what
the author intends to express at the moment." Yerushalmi's literal translation follows:

> Son who is dear to me, Shelomoh. In the seventh of the days of the years of
> your life the Spirit of the Lord began to move you and spoke within you:
> Go, read in my Book that I have written and there will burst open for you
> the wellsprings of understanding, knowledge, and wisdom. Behold, it is the
> Book of Books, from which sages have excavated and lawmakers learned
> knowledge and judgement. A vision of the Almighty did you see; you heard
> and strove to do, and you soared on the wings of the Spirit.
>
> Since then the book has been stored like the fragments of the tablets
> in an ark with me. For the day on which your years were filled to five and
> thirty I have put upon it a cover of new skin and have called it: "Spring up,
> O well, sing ye unto it!" And I have presented it to you as a memorial and as
> a reminder of love from your father, who loves you with an everlasting love.
>
> Jakob Son of R. Shelomoh Freid [sic]
> In the capital city of Vienna 29 Nisan [5]651 6 May [1]891[19]

Evidently, the Philippson bible is meant not only to remind Freud
of his father's love but also to recall him to the God of his Fathers. Jacob's
inscription clearly encodes a gentle rebuke to his son about his immer-
sion in gentile culture. Of particular interest is the following verse: "Since
then the book has been stored like the fragments of the tablets in an ark
with me." The fragments in question are those of the tables of the law,
smashed by Moses when he descended from Sinai and found his people
worshiping the golden calf. As Yerushalmi points out, the tradition that
the broken tablets were stored in the ark is not biblical but talmudic.[20]
Jacob Freud's simile, which implicitly places his wayward son in the position of idolater, may have in mind not only Sigmund's general attraction
to gentile culture but, even more specifically, his famous collection of
antiquities, which included many Egyptian as well as classical (and some
Jewish) objects.[21] From his father's perspective, Freud was quite literally
an idol-worshiper, collecting images of gods that were forbidden by
Mosaic law. Thus the simile records both Moses' anger when he smashes
the tables and the gesture of atonement when the fragments are saved
and re-presented in the form of the family bible. More generally, Jacob's
inscription revives a traditional set of oppositions in which paternity,
Jewishness, and the (biblical) text are set against maternity, the gentile,
and the image.

Within this clear structure, however, the Philippson bible is a much more ambiguous object than Jacob Freud's inscription would suggest. For the generous woodcuts, often taken from Egyptian subjects, reintroduce into the Hebrew scriptures those very images that fall under the Mosaic ban. The Egyptian gods I reproduced for this chapter, for instance, are used to illustrate Deuteronomy 4, which sternly elaborates the warnings against idolatry. Thus Philippson's commentary restores, as commentary, the same transgressive objects that the text itself has just forbidden.[22] (Philippson himself was no absolutist on matters of religion. He pursued part of his studies at a Protestant school and evinced a passion for Germanic mythology.[23]) Philippson produces something not unlike the "superior" Moses that Freud imagined he found in Michelangelo's statue (*S.E.* 13: 233). Just as Michelangelo's Moses restrains himself from smashing the Tables of the Law, and by countenancing idolatry implicitly justifies Michelangelo's own "graven image," so Philippson creates a bible in which the proscription against images nevertheless allows a place for them.[24]

For Freud, the Philippson bible functioned less as a call to Jewish orthodoxy than as a reminder of the Egyptian (maternal) imaginary of his youth. In fact, the father's gift of the rebound bible in 1891 seems to have inspired Sigmund to interpret his childhood anxiety dream. Gérard Huber argues, using the chronology Freud himself gives, that this childhood dream, rather than the celebrated one of Irma's injection, is actually the first that Freud analyzed, and that it is therefore not without reason that Freud describes *The Interpretation of Dreams* in a letter to Fliess as his "Egyptian dream book."[25] If Freud's chronology is correct (and some scholars have challenged it), then the restoration of the Philippson bible, with its storehouse of Egyptian/maternal imagery, helped spark a creative surge in Freud very much like the one Leonardo experienced when (as Freud surmises) he encountered his mother's smile on the face of Mona Lisa del Giocondo. Far from recalling him to his Jewish roots, his father's gift has the unintended effect of reviving Freud's childhood idolatry.

If we stop and take stock of our argument to this point, we find that the Egyptian imaginary signifies two things for Freud. The first is an idolatrous falling-off from both a Hebraic sublime and his father's approval. The second, in the Leonardo book, is a maternally imposed homosexuality. But the conjunction of these two themes lands us right back at the first chapter of Romans, with the difference that Egypt has taken the pace of Greece. Freud's "rewriting" of Romans 1 (which is not cited in the Leonardo book) runs as follows: Because you have abandoned the unrepresentable Hebrew deity for Egyptian images, and thus substituted a maternal identification for a paternal one, you (Leonardo? Freud?) are fated to become a homosexual.[26]

Yet to put it this way is to insist on Freud's distance from St. Paul. For the latter, Greek homosexuality is imposed by a vengeful paternal God, while Freudian homosexuality results precisely from the absence (or attenuation) of paternal agency. For Freud, moreover, there is no causal connection between idolatry and homosexuality. Both are mere signifiers or effects of an overwhelming maternal presence that has deflected a more normative oedipal trajectory. And for these reasons, Freud empties out (or at least complicates) Paul's understanding of homosexuality as *punishment*. For Freud, Leonardo's homosexuality is not, in itself, an affliction, but it is the consequence of a prior violence—the mother's traumatic, vulture-like attacks on her infant son. Like Shakespeare, then, Freud is an ambiguously subversive inheritor of the Pauline legacy. While he manages to evacuate the language of divine punishment and condemnation, he nevertheless reproduces a displaced version of Paul's logic.

*   *   *

From the start, then, Egyptian imagery exists for Freud in tension with the Hebraic sublime that is supposed to annihilate and supplant it. As Freud notes in *Moses and Monotheism*, "the contrast between the Mosaic and the Egyptian religions is a deliberate one and has been intentionally heightened" (*S.E.* 23:19); that is, the Mosaic religion defines itself as the negation of its Egyptian counterpart. Yet this negation is never thoroughly carried through, and so Egypt persists as a kind of transgressive maternal remnant in the face of its paternal antagonist. Moreover, this contest has an obvious aesthetic dimension in addition to its psychic and cultural ones. Tracing its affinities to Hegel's treatment of sublime and Egyptian art in his *Aesthetics* will help clarify the aesthetic contours of the Freudian sublime.

Hegel's treatment of sublime art occurs in a larger section on symbolism; indeed, it divides, in a manner suggestive for psychoanalysis, the symbolic mode between its "unconscious" (*unbewusste*) and "conscious" variants. By "unconscious symbolism" Hegel points not to a repressed content but rather to symbolism that is spontaneous or unself-conscious, unable to grasp itself *as* symbol. It is the product of relatively primitive "Eastern" religions that take given, natural objects as symbols of the divine. In this mode, the mind cannot separate abstract meaning from artistic content, and so grasps them as an immediate unity. The aesthetic labor performed by the sublime, as embodied in Hebrew scripture, is to detach spirit or absolute meaning from its concrete expression. It does this by positing a God who exists apart from, and remains unrepresentable by, the natural world he has created. The sublime thus establishes a purely negative relation between meaning and content, but in so doing prepares the way for the deliberate, self-aware activity of comparison that marks conscious symbolism. Freud similarly holds that the Jewish ban on images "meant that a sensory perception was given second place to what may be called an abstract idea" (*S.E.* 23: 113).

For Hegel, as for Freud, the immediate precursor of the Hebrew sublime is Egyptian art, in which unconscious symbolism achieves its highest development. "Egypt is the country of symbols, the country that sets itself the spiritual task of the self-decipherment of spirit, without actually attaining to the decipherment" (354). In Egypt, it might be said, symbolism does not yet become conscious, but the unconsciousness of symbolism becomes visible and provokes an endless and fruitless labor of decipherment. The form proper to this frozen or paralyzed self-analysis of symbol is the riddle: "In this sense we regard the Egyptian work of art as containing riddles, the right solution of which is unattained not only by us, but generally by those who posed the riddles to themselves" (360). As riddle, Egyptian art unleashes a "Freudian" displacement of meaning: "In Egypt, on the whole, almost every shape is a symbol and hieroglyph not signifying itself but hinting at another thing with which it has affinity and therefore relationship" (357). Conversely, Freud grasps the artwork through the "Egyptian" categories of riddle or enigma.[27] And nowhere in Freud's writing does the enigmatic or riddling quality of the artwork appear as insistently as in the Leonardo book. Leonardo himself is an "enigma" (63) whose "attitude toward his art remained a riddle" (66). But it is in relation to the *Mona Lisa* that this theme reaches its highest pitch. Freud quotes the (aptly named) critic R. Muther, who states that "no one has solved the riddle of her smile, no one has read the meaning of her thoughts," as well as the critic E. Müntz, who describes the *Mona Lisa* as an "énigme indéchiffrable" (108). As such, the *Mona Lisa* is the legitimate offspring of Leonardo's Egyptian/maternal phantasy.

Although Egyptian art does not achieve the radical negativity of the Hebrew sublime, it does apprehend the negative, Hegel argues, through the concepts of death and of the immortality of the human soul. "With them, that is, there first emerges in this higher way . . . the separation between nature and spirit" (355). Egyptian art is thus an art of death, symbolized in the pyramids and in the practice of embalming, through which "the dead acquires the content of the living itself. Deprived of immediate existence, the dead still preserves its relation to the living, and in this concrete shape it is made independent and maintained. . . . The honour paid to the dead by the Egyptians is not burial, but their perennial preservation as corpses." Egyptian art is thus an art of encryption. Both Freud's childhood dream and his treatment of Leonardo's art sustain this connection (as does the image of the Egyptian tomb in Wilde's *Portrait of Mr. W.H.*) but specify the encrypted or preserved object as the mother.

These "Hegelian" themes of the riddle and the crypt converge in Freud's reading of the *St. Anne with Two Others*—or rather, in a subsequent elaboration of this reading that Freud includes in a later footnote. Here, of course, I refer to the Swiss analyst Oskar Pfister's notorious "discovery" of a vulture-image in Leonardo's painting. In a footnote added in 1919, Freud reproduces a drawing from an article of Pfister's that claims to show that the folds of Mary's drapery form the shape of a vulture, whose tail, moreover, ends in the infant Jesus's mouth—thus exactly reproducing Leonardo's childhood fantasy (see Figure 2). Freud remained imperfectly convinced of Pfister's claim but found it sufficiently plausible to annex it to his own work.[28] Pfister's contribution not only reinforces Freud's thesis about Egypt, maternity, and Leonardo's art but also engages, and indeed condenses, the "Hegelian" themes I have just been tracing. For not only does Pfister describe his vulture-discovery as a "picture-puzzle" (*Vexierbild*), and thus invoke the "Egyptian" theme of the riddle or enigma, but he includes it in a section of his article devoted to what he calls "cryptography" (*Kryptographie*).[29] Since it is the encrypted image that renders Leonardo's painting a "puzzle" or riddle, the two Hegelian motifs become one. Together, Pfister and Freud do far more than locate Egyptian mythology in the content of Leonardo's art;

Figure 2. Oskar Pfister, "Kryptolalie, Kryptographie und unbewusstes Vexierbild bei Normalen," *Jahrbuch für Psychoanalytische und Psychopathologische Forschungen* 5 (1913). Photograph courtesy of the Butler Library, Columbia University.

they relocate the art itself and its formal aspects into the realm of an "Egyptian" aesthetic.

Pfister's "discovery" has an eerie power that seems to be enhanced rather than dispelled by the fact that it is undeniably an hallucination. Any encounter with the drawing makes it henceforth almost impossible *not* to "see" the vulture in Leonardo's painting—a visual equivalent of the bad song one can't get out of one's head. Moreover, the form as well as the content of the image render it striking. The vulture is immediately recognizable because of its crude, cartoonish outline. Like a residue from some archaic representational system, it sits undigested in the midst of Leonardo's painting—a hieroglyph, perhaps. Indeed, the "encrypted" quality of the vulture seems to depend in part on this formal disjunction. The vulture does not occupy the representational depth of the painting but rather is splayed flatly across the surface of the canvas, at once obvious and invisible through its contrast with Leonardo's famously subtle brushwork. The vulture persists as the dead leftover of a representational regime that the rest of the painting has surpassed. It does not harmonize with its pictorial surroundings but bursts forth, absurd and incongruous, like the return of the repressed. Similarly, Leonardo's encrypted mother manifests herself as the crudely sexual vulture-phantasy and as the disturbingly sublime smile on Leonardo's otherwise reassuringly maternal figures. If it is objected that the drawing at issue here is Pfister's and not Freud's, I would respond that the ambiguous status of the drawing— included but banished to the exterior intimacy of the footnote, reproduced but not endorsed by Freud, presented but not fully digested or assimilated—simply redoubles the problems I have been discussing. Pfister's drawing is to Freud's Leonardo book what the encrypted vulture is to Leonardo's *St. Anne with Two Others*.[30]

In connection with Freud's analysis, moreover, the drawing radically reinterprets Renaissance art so that it is seen not as the evolutionary rebirth of classical forms but as the abrupt recrudescence of Egypt—an "Egyptian" Renaissance based on traumatic repetition of forbidden hieroglyphs rather than a dialogical engagement with official models of beauty. At the heart of Leonardo's painting, a bizarre, inverted vulture. Freud's art history thus seems to undo the apparently "progressivist" narrative of Hegel's—or rather it would, were it not for the fact that the Egyptian art of embalming, which preserves but suspends its object, already offers a frozen parody of the Hegelian *Aufhebung*, and thus registers within Hegel's discourse a tendency for the repressed to return and for the canceled to persist, uncannily, even beyond the limits of its dialectical sublation.

* * *

Leonardo da Vinci and a Memory of His Childhood is Freud's most extended and systematic unfolding of the concept of sublimation. But by virtue of that fact it throws the fissures and contradictions of the concept into sharper relief. In one of his seminars on sublimation, Jean Laplanche notes that "from the beginning to the end [of Freud's corpus], sublimation will be cited more than it is developed and analyzed: it serves less as a concept than as an index of a questioning that must be played out, a task to be achieved, an indispensable notion but one that is never "grasped" in its *Begriff*."[31] Laplanche does an admirable job, nevertheless, of working out the metapsychological niceties of sublimation. What I am concerned with here is rather the way in which the narrative structures of the Leonardo book help both to form and to frame the concept.

In one sense, sublimation serves as a limit of thought rather than a concept. Freud is able to trace the paths of Leonardo's sublimations, and he makes a valiant if incoherent effort to distinguish sublimation from the return of the repressed, but what he cannot do is explain why Leonardo (or anyone else) is capable of sublimation as opposed to some more overtly pathological form of psychic defense.[32] "We are left, then," Freud admits at the end of his study, "with these two characteristics of Leonardo that are inexplicable by the efforts of psycho-analysis: his quite special tendency towards instinctual repressions, and his extraordinary capacity for sublimating the primitive instincts" (136). One of the complexities of Freud's study is that Leonardo follows two different sublimatory paths. He turns his infantile scopophilia toward art and painting and his infantile sexual researches toward scientific investigation. But while both of these activities originate in the same pre-oedipal milieu, they become incompatible and even somewhat antagonistic. Leonardo's scientific endeavors, originally undertaken to make him a more knowledgeable and expert artist, consume more and more of his time and eventually cause him to neglect painting. "The artist had once taken the investigator into his service to assist him; now the servant had become the stronger and suppressed his master" (77). The conflict between artist and scientist particularly interests Freud, since it forms one of the bases for his identification with Leonardo.

Although the choice of sublimation over repression remains something of a mystery, one of its crucial enabling conditions in Leonardo's case was the move from his mother's to his grandfather's household—at age five according to Freud. Living with his father allows Leonardo to achieve a paternal identification, though belated and secondary with respect to his maternal one. Ser Piero's influence does not arrive in time to have any effect on Leonardo's sexuality, but "his identification with his father ... nevertheless continued in other spheres of non-erotic activity" (121), particularly art and science. Soon Leonardo acquires additional, supplementary father figures: the artist Verrocchio, in whose shop he was apprenticed, and later his patron the duke of Milan: "he passed through a period of masculine creative power and artistic productiveness in Milan, where a kindly fate enabled him to find a father-substitute in the Duke Lodovico Moro" (133). As the phrase "masculine creative power" (*männlicher Schaffenskraft*; *G.W.* 8: 206) suggests, Leonardo's artistic achievements derive from his paternal identification. Sublimation in the psychoanalytic sense thus rejoins its original, alchemical significance as a defeminizing process, a purging of maternal influence. While the energizing phantasy behind his greatest paintings is clearly maternal and pre-oedipal, the ability to turn this phantasy into art rests squarely on Leonardo's paternal identification, and on a distancing from the mother. "There is no doubt," Freud states, "that the creative artist feels towards his works like a father" (121). At the same time, however, Leonardo's identification with this *particular* father also inhibits his art. "He created [his paintings] and then cared no more about them, just as his father had not cared about him" (121). Leonardo's later neglect of painting results not only from the competing demands of science, then, but also from an inhibitory element *within* his paternal identification and hence within the artistic sublimation itself.

"But if his imitation of his father did him damage as an artist, his rebellion against his father was the infantile determinant of what was perhaps an equally sublime [*grossartigen*] achievement in the field of scientific research" (122). Specifically, Leonardo turns his rebellion against his father's authority into independence of scholarly authority, and thus becomes the first man since the time of the Greeks to probe the secrets of nature while relying solely on observation and his own judgment. But in teaching that authority should be looked down on and that imitation of the "ancients" should be repudiated, and in constantly urging that the study of nature was the source of all truth, he was merely repeating—in the highest sublimation attainable by man—the one-sided point of view which had already forced itself on the little boy as he gazed in wonder on the world. If we translate scientific abstraction back into concrete individual experience, we see that the "ancients" and authority simply correspond to the father, and nature once more becomes the tender and kindly mother who had nourished him. (122)

Leonardo's scientific research, like his painting, thus involves a maternal content and a paternal form. If his investigations into nature seem to arise from an oedipal rebellion against the father rather than an identification with him, it is nevertheless true that "When, at the climax of a discovery, he could survey a large portion of the whole nexus, he was overcome by emotion, and in ecstatic language praised the splendour of the part of creation he had studied, or—in religious phraseology—the greatness of his Creator" (75). Independence of the paternal force known as scholarly authority thus culminates in pious reverence toward the divine Father—a kind of hymn or psalm, like those that Hegel finds characteristic of the Hebrew sublime.

Freud does not map Leonardo's movement from painting to science on an ascending line, however. Instead, he emphasizes the increasing price that Leonardo's sublimations and sexual renunciations exact, and he sees his career as succumbing to greater inhibitions and frustrations. As Bradley Collins points out, Freud contrasts

Leonardo's nonneurotic artistic activity with his "obsessional" and "regressive" scientific researches. Art is an outgrowth of "masculine creative power" that brings Leonardo material success and the world's acclaim (133). During his artistically productive years in Milan, Leonardo is "radiantly productive and pleasure-loving" (65). He glides through Milanese circles as someone who was "charming in his manner, supremely eloquent, and cheerful and amiable to everyone" (64). The pursuit of science, however, makes him overdeliberate, inhibited, and cut off from society. His researches are driven by infantile impulses characterized by their "insatiability, unyielding rigidity and the lack of an ability to adapt to real circumstances" (133). In the throes of his urge to investigate, "the sparkle of his temperament may have grown dim." (65)[33]

Collins nicely captures the general contours of Freud's narrative, but he slightly misrepresents the argument made by Freud, who posits Leonardo's turn from art to science as the effect, not the cause, of an increasing inhibition that also afflicts the painting. Freud describes the transition from art to science as part of a larger regressive movement:

> Slowly there occurred in him a process which can only be compared to the regressions in neurotics. The development that turned him into an artist at puberty was overtaken by the process which led him to be an investigator, and which had its determinants in early infancy. The second sublimation of his erotic instinct gave place to the original sublimation for which the way had been prepared on the occasion of the first repression. He became an investigator, at first still in the service of his art, but later independently of it and away from it. With the loss of his patron, the substitute for his father, and with the increasingly somber colors which his life took on, this regressive shift assumed larger and larger proportions. (133)

Although it is not described as a function of this, Leonardo's regression is certainly deepened by the loss of a father-figure and, one assumes, the subsequent weakening of that paternal identification that underlay his artistic productiveness. But Leonardo's artistic career is then saved by a new and surprising development:

> At the summit of his life, when he was in his early fifties—a time when in women the sexual characters have already undergone involution and when in men the libido not infrequently makes a further energetic advance—a new transformation came over him. Still deeper layers of the contents of his mind became active once more; but this further regression was to the benefit of his art, which was in the process of becoming stunted. He met the woman who awakened the memory of his mother's happy smile of sensual rapture; and, influenced by this revived memory, he recovered the stimulus that guided him at the beginning of his artistic endeavors, at the time when he modelled the smiling women. He painted the Mona Lisa, the "St. Anne with Two Others" and the series of mysterious pictures which are characterized by the enigmatic smile. With the help of the oldest of all his erotic impulses he enjoyed the triumph of once more conquering the inhibition in his art. (133–34)

Leonardo's art is saved, then, not because he halts or reverses the regressive trend that had inhibited it but because the regression drives itself all the way back to his original, pre-oedipal state. His life takes on a comic rather than a tragic shape when an Odyssean circularity causes him to end up where he began.

Yet the allusion to Homer is misleading, for a very different literary paradigm organizes Freud's book. Leonardo begins in the mother's house, the space both of pre-oedipal desire (and trauma) and of the Egyptian imaginary with which it is intimately bound up. At age five, Leonardo is transferred from the mother's to the father's (and grand-father's) household, thus provoking the sublimations that bring him worldly and artistic success. In moving away from the mother, Leonardo also escapes his pleasant but devastating subjection to maternal demand and enters a patriarchal household in which he comes to assert his autonomy. A journey, then, from enslavement to freedom, from pre-oedipal confinement to patriarchal sublimation, from Egypt to the Land of his Fathers.

And yet Leonardo's Israel is not a land of milk and honey. After his youthful triumphs, he is burdened by the renunciations under which he labors and begins to long for the fleshpots of Egypt. Is he in Israel, after all, or the long desert journey of Exodus? In any case, his psychic development begins the long regression that will eventually take him all the way back to his mother's house and its bird-headed gods. Not surprisingly, this regression will usher in the triumph of his artistic career, devoted to framing encrypted images of the old deities.

Leonardo's career is thus a narrative of failed Exodus, an imaginary history in which the decisive crossing from Egypt to Palestine (and hence, not incidentally, from the realm of the image to that of the sublime) is reversed. Leonardo's regression from oedipal father to pre-oedipal mother may recall Shakespeare's strategy in Sonnet 20, when he replaces God the Father with maternal Nature in his rewriting of the Genesis myth. The parallel is even more striking if we accept Ilse Barande's reading of *St. Anne with Two Others* as a feminizing of the Holy Trinity, with Anne taking the place of God the Father.[34] Both Leonardo and Shakespeare would, in that instance, invoke a sublime paternal deity only to turn away from it toward an aesthetics of the beautiful. Unlike Shakespeare, however, Leonardo cannot escape so easily from the sublime, since even the mother is, for him, edged with the memory of trauma. The best he can do is regress from a paternal sublime to a maternal one—subtly terrifying in the *Mona Lisa*, more peaceable and blissful in the *Heilige Anna Selbdritt*.

Leonardo's path is all the more resonant in that the contours of his personal history come to resemble those of the culture at large. In *Moses and Monotheism*, Freud has the following to say about the birth of Christianity:

> In some respects the new religion meant a cultural regression as compared with the older Jewish one.... The Christian religion did not maintain the high level in things of the mind to which Judaism had soared. It was no longer strictly monotheist, it took over numerous symbolic rituals from the surrounding peoples, it re-established the great mother goddess and found room to introduce many of the divine figures of polytheism only lightly veiled, though in subordinate positions. (*S.E.* 23: 88)

Leonardo's life enacts in little the history of religion as Freud understands it, moving from Egyptian polytheism to Jewish monotheism and then suffering a regression from the oedipal father to the pre-oedipal mother. To make the parallel all the clearer, Freud adds that "The triumph of Christianity was a fresh victory for the priests of Amun over Akhenaten's god after an interval of fifteen hundred years and on a wider stage" (*S.E.* 23: 88). That is to say, Christianity is a return of the *Egyptian* repressed within the field of monotheism. Christianity is thus itself a failure or betrayal of Exodus, a hankering after the abandoned maternal gods and their images. If Oskar Pfister's drawing appealed to Freud on some level, it must have been because it not only supported the latter's theory of Leonardo but, by situating the Egyptian vulture goddess in the midst of Christian art, imaged forth Freud's own developing intuitions about the shape of religious and cultural history. Christianity contains Leonardo's Egyptian Renaissance writ large.

If Leonardo's is a life marked by regression, it is nevertheless heavy with futurity in the sense that it foreshadows many of the themes of Freud's later work, not only in *Moses and Monotheism* but also in *Civilization and Its Discontents*, a book that, like the one on Leonardo, explores the high price to be paid for sexual renunciation. Here too Leonardo's personal pathologies get reworked into the dilemmas of culture as such. All of which raises an interesting question: what about the other elements in Leonardo's life that aren't so reworked, particularly those of the maternal superego and its relation to Leonardo's homo-sexuality? Mightn't these contain the seeds of a counter-mythology to Freud's dominant oedipal narrative? If Leonardo's history is also Freudian History, might his life not prophesy, in typological fashion, the homosexualization of culture? Leonardo's vulture, translator's error and Freudian phantasm, would then spread its wings over us all.

CHAPTER FOUR

Lacan's Anal Thing:
The Ethics of Psychoanalysis

Jacques Lacan's Seventh Seminar, *The Ethics of Psychoanalysis*, introduces his concept of *das Ding* or the Thing and employs it to elaborate a distinctive theory of ethics. At the end of a long section on sublimation, which he redefines as the raising of an object to "the dignity of the Thing" (112),[1] Lacan adds a "Supplementary Note" showing that sublimation, as he defines it, does *not* necessarily desexualize its objects. "Far from it; the sexual object acknowledged as such may come to light in sublimation. The crudest of sexual games can be the object of a poem without for that reason losing its sublimating goal" (161). Because he has been discussing sublimation in the context of courtly love poetry, Lacan proves his point by analyzing a lyric by the twelfth-century langue d'oc poet Arnaut Daniel, renowned for his elaborate rhyme schemes and stanzaic forms. Like much courtly love poetry, this lyric involves a Lady or *Domna* who imposes a test on her lover. The narrator of the poem, however, cannot condone the unusual challenge that Lady Ena has devised for Lord Bernart. Here is a prose translation of the first three stanzas:

> Though Lord Raimond, in agreement with Lord Truc Malec, defends Lady Ena and her orders, I would grow old and white before I would consent to a request that involves so great an impropriety. For so as "to put his mouth to her trumpet," he would need the kind of beak that could pick grain out of a pipe. And even then he might come out blind, as the smoke from those folds is so strong.
>
> He would need a beak and a long, sharp one, for the trumpet is rough, ugly and hairy, and it is never dry, and the swamp within is deep. That is why pitch ferments upward as it continually escapes, continually overflows. And it is not fitting that he who puts his mouth to that pipe be a favorite.
>
> There will be plenty of other tests, finer ones that are worth far more, and if Lord Bernart withdrew from that one, he did not, by Christ, behave

like a coward if he was taken with fear and fright. For if the stream of water had landed on him from above, it would have scalded his whole cheek and neck, and it is not fitting also that a lady embrace a man who has blown a stinking trumpet. (162)[2]

As I shall argue, Arnaut's odd lyric is crucial to Lacan's concepts of *das Ding* and of sublimation, and it elucidates important tenets of Lacanian ethics as well.[3]

Before turning to this topic, however, I want to mention an almost parenthetical remark that occurs near the end of this supplementary note. After discussing the poem, Lacan says: "I wouldn't tell all if I didn't add to the file, in case it proves useful, that Dante places Arnaud Daniel in Canto XIV of his *Purgatory* in the company of sodomites" (163). Lacan's remark is all the more intriguing in that it contains a couple of imprecisions. First, Arnaut Daniel appears in Canto XXVI of the *Purgatorio*, not Canto XIV.[4] Second, Dante does *not* include Daniel among the sodomites of *Purgatorio* XXVI. This particular circle of Purgatory contains two classes of sinners, circling in opposite directions. The members of one line cry out "Sodom and Gomorrah," while the others cry "Pasiphaë enters into the cow, that the bull may hasten to her lust" (*Purg.* XXVI, 40–42).[5] Arnaut Daniel is a member of this second group, whose sin is described as "ermafrodito" (*Purg.* XXVI, 82), a term used here to *distinguish* it from sodomy by implying the union of two sexes. While the name Pasiphaë invokes bestiality, the actual sin seems to entail only a "bestial" excess of sexual indulgence. The followers of Pasiphaë share with the sodomites an unnatural sexuality, and their identification with a woman who is mounted from behind certainly suggests other similarities. Nevertheless, while Arnaut Daniel might be said to be "in the company of sodomites" insofar as he occupies a circle of Purgatory with them (members of the two lines greet and kiss one other as they pass), he is clearly not *classed* as a sodomite, *pace* Lacan. Like Freud's mistranslation of *nibbio*, however, Lacan's error will prove to be a productive one, affiliating sodomy all the more deeply with his concept of sublimation.

Before tracing these connections, however, we will have to tour the conceptual apparatus of Lacan's seminar up to this point, beginning with *das Ding*. The Freudian unconscious, as understood by Lacan, is a chain of representations or *Vorstellungen* governed by the pleasure principle, which articulates excitations (both internal and external) into this chain so as to maintain the subject's internal homeostasis. Lacan defines the "good" of classical ethics as pertaining to the pleasure principle—the "good" is what brings pleasure, or reduces tension within the subject. An object is "good" or "bad" insofar as it bears qualitative attributes that form part of the chain of unconscious representations and submit the object to the pleasure principle. By contrast, a first definition of the "Thing" would be that aspect of an object which does not lend itself to psychic representation—a pure, irreducible alterity that remains "beyond" the pleasure principle. As developed by Lacan, the Thing is a kind of unbearable, terrible Good whose incandescence is also therefore an Evil. The mother, insofar as she is at once the object of incestuous desire and forbidden by the prohibition on incest, occupies the position of the Thing, though it cannot be said that the mother "is" the Thing. (70). Leonardo's *Mona Lisa*, whose smile betokens an overwhelming, traumatic demand, shines with the sublime light of the maternal Thing.

For Lacan, the Thing is so exterior (yet so intimate) to the logic of the subject that it is not even repressed; it is rather "a primordial function which is located at the level of the initial establishment of the gravitational center of the unconscious *Vorstellungen*" (62), thereby orienting the field of the real for the subject. As the lost object around which "the whole field of the *Vorstellungen* turns" (57), *das Ding* cannot itself be represented, nor can it appear directly. It manifests itself only as the virtual center around which the *Vorstellungen* revolve. In this sense, "the Thing only presents itself to the extent that it becomes word" (55), that is, only as a function of the network of signifiers that circle around it.

Lacan defines sublimation in a way that follows directly from this. "The object is elevated to the dignity of the Thing as we define it in our Freudian topology insofar as it is not slipped into but surrounded by the network of *Ziele*" (112). While Freudian sublimation deflects the drive from a sexual to a nonsexual aim, Lacanian sublimation removes the object of the drive from the system of aims (*Ziele*) entirely, placing it instead at that empty gravitational center which is the Thing. This newly "aimless" object already recalls the Kantian definition of the artwork, and Lacan illustrates the process of sublimation almost exclusively with examples of literary and visual art. The very first extended example of sublimation cited in the seminar is Jacques Prévert's collection of empty, interlocked matchboxes. By being joined in a (potentially) infinite but pointless series, these formerly useful objects become "wholly gratuitous, proliferating, superfluous, and quasi-absurd" (114). Lacanian sublimation thus pushes Kantian purposelessness to its surrealist limit; its perfect embodiment might well be the Duchampian ready-made.

Yet for Lacan, *all* art incorporates a void that signifies its approach to the Thing: "This thing will always be represented by emptiness, precisely because it cannot be represented by anything else—or more exactly, because it can only be represented by something else. But in every form of sublimation, emptiness is determinative.... All art is characterized by a certain mode of organization around this emptiness" (129–30), whether the literal emptiness of Jacques Prévert's matchboxes, or the vital emptiness of the anamorphic skull (itself a stain or hole in the fabric of representation) in Holbein's *Ambassadors* (135), or the spiritual emptiness of Lady Ena in Arnaut Daniel's poem.

As his emphasis on "raising" or "elevating" the object would suggest, Lacan's understanding of art as sublimation has less to do with Freud directly than it does with the concept of the sublime. What is at stake is always an attempt to represent the unrepresentable Thing. "The fact is that man fashions this signifier and introduces it into the world—in other words, ... he fashions it in the image of the Thing, whereas the Thing is characterized by the fact that it is impossible for us to imagine it" (125). Lacan's formulations throughout the Seventh Seminar are imbued with theological depth, and here he clearly glances at the Hebrew prohibition against idolatry.[6] But if the artwork is a profaning attempt to fashion an image in the shape of the invisible, it also carries its own iconoclasm within it: "At issue, in an analogical or anamorphic form, is the effort to point once again to the fact that what we seek in the illusion is something in which the illusion as such in some way transcends itself, destroys itself, by demonstrating that it is only there as a signifier" (136). For Lacan, every artwork is a broken image, achieving sublime revelation through the shards of its failed idolatry.

Sublimity is clearly at play in the chapter entitled "On Creation *ex nihilo*," which combines a disquisition on the Heideggerian Thing with the narrative of divine creation in Genesis. Lacan's paradigm for creation is the fashioning of a vessel or "vase," his counterpart to the jug in Heidegger's famous essay, "The Thing."[7] Distinguishing between the vase's "signifying function and its use as a utensil," Lacan argues that the vase "is in its signifying essence a signifier of nothing other than signifying as such, or in other words, of no particular signified." Moreover, "this nothing in particular that characterizes its signifying function is that which in its incarnated form characterizes the vase as such. It creates the void and thereby introduces the possibility of filling it." (120). So the vase's physical emptiness, the void it creates by surrounding it, allegorizes its own status as empty signifier, a signifier of nothing. A vase is created ex nihilo insofar as it is organized around the emptiness at its center, and in this regard it is like any other artwork, "an object made to represent the existence of the emptiness at the center of the Real that is called the Thing" (121). Yet, as Lacan says, the vase also "creates the void"; thus it is not only creation *from* nothing but (even more fundamentally) creation *of* nothing, since the void that is the *vase's* void cannot precede it. Once again the vase allegorizes signification as such, insofar as "the fashioning of the signifier and the introduction of a gap or a hole in the real is identical" (121). The real is a plenum that does not allow of absence or loss; only a symbolic system can incise the real, divide it up, and offer the emptiness of an unfilled slot or position.[8] Lacanian creation thus offers a photographic negative of divine creation in Genesis, since it opens a void from within the fulness of the real. It is, however, very much like Blakean creation as described in *The Marriage of Heaven and Hell*: "But first the notion that man has a body separate from his soul, is to be expunged; this I shall do, by printing in the infernal method, by corrosives, which in Hell are salutary and medicinal, melting apparent surfaces away, and displaying the infinite that was hid."[9] Blake's image of writing or poetic creation as the eating away or annihilation of matter refers both to his somewhat antiquated technique of "relief etching," in which acid or burin cut directly into copper plates, and to the corrosive of satire.[10] Lacan seems to engage in his own "diabolical" revision of scripture, at once alluding to creation from the divine Word and inverting the sense of that creation.

Similarly diabolical notions underlie Lacan's choice to cite and analyze the disturbing poem by Arnaut Daniel, which not only throws a lurid light on the conventions of courtly love poetry but—as we shall see—completes the insidious revision of Heidegger which Lacan begins in the "ex nihilo" chapter. In one sense, Lady Ena is the typical mistress of the love lyric as described by Lacan, for "in this poetic field the feminine object is emptied of all real substance" (149). Cruel and inaccessible, devoid of any real or concrete virtues, she is "an object I can only describe as terrifying, an inhuman partner" (150). If Lady Ena differs from her poetic sorority, it is only in presenting this emptiness in an especially coarse and bodily fashion:

> The idealized woman, the Lady, who is in the position of the Other and of the object, finds herself suddenly and brutally positing, in a place knowingly constructed out of the most refined of signifiers, the emptiness of a thing in all its crudity, a thing that reveals itself in its nudity to be the thing, her thing, the one that is to be found at her very heart in its cruel emptiness. That Thing, whose function certain of you perceived in the relation to sublimation, is in a way unveiled with a cruel and insistent power. (163)

The Lady's emptiness may well be that of her "cruel heart," but this spiritual emptiness finds its counterpart in the "trumpet" on which she asks her admirer to blow. The Lady's "thing" is therefore the anus, an aperture which, far more than the vagina (traditional signifier of castration), seems suited to embodying the emptiness of the Thing as such. Why is this? Let us return to Lacan's almost parenthetical allusion to sodomy at the end of his discussion of the poem. As I noted in my first chapter, medieval discourse on sodomy referred to the anus as the "improper vessel," to distinguish it from the vagina as the "proper" vessel for receiving the male seed. The Latin term was *vas* (or *vasum*) *indebitum* or, more rarely, *vas* (or *vasum*) *improprium*.[11] Here I want to focus on the less common term, which is closer to the English translation and brings out an important figurative dimension. In the phobic terms of anti-sodomy discourse, the anus is an "improper" vessel not only in the obvious sense that it is the wrong one of the two but in the more fundamental sense that it fails to fulfill its purpose *as* vessel. Here we might invoke Heidegger's understanding of the vessel in his essay on "The Thing" as a "holding vessel" (*das fassende Gefäss*), an object whose essential function is to contain what is placed within it.[12] The anus is an "improper" vessel because, while it *surrounds* the seed left inside, it cannot *hold* it as the uterus can; that is, it cannot provide the kind of "holding" that the nature of the seed as seed requires. The anus is an improper vessel for that which it finds inside; and therefore, no matter how much is deposited within it, it remains in some sense "empty." For the discourse of sodomy, the anus is the paradigmatically empty space, the vessel as absolute void.

Keeping this in mind, let us return to the chapter "On Creation *ex nihilo*" and consider the ways in which Lacan revises the Heideggerian Thing. Heidegger's project in his essay is to approach the "thingness" of things, their Being as opposed to their function or utility. To this end he chooses a jug (*der Krug*) and begins by focusing on its emptiness, as does Lacan. For Heidegger, however, the emptiness of the jug is largely a prologue, first to its taking and keeping of what is poured into it, and then to the even more essential moment of a libational pouring out: "Nevertheless, the taking of what was poured in and the keeping of what was poured belong together. But their unity is determined by the outpouring for which the jug is fitted as a jug.... We call the gathering of the twofold holding into the outpouring, which as a being together, first constitutes the full presence of giving: the poured gift" (171–72). It is this gift of outpouring that fully manifests the being or Thingness of the jug, by a fourfold marrying of earth and sky, mortals and gods. In the moment of outpouring, the gift that gushes forth is not just the libation but also the Thingness of the thing, its Being.

Lacan's Thing shares with Heidegger's a nature that is at once proximate and distant, essentially veiled and furtive but also epiphanic. Yet Lacan's "vase" is very different from Heidegger's jug, because Lacan adheres only to the initial Heideggerian moment of emptiness. Thus where Heidegger notes that "even the empty jug retains its nature by virtue of the poured gift" (172), Lacan conversely insists that "if the vase may be filled, it is because in the first place in its essence it is empty" (120). This is not to deny that the jug as emptiness or void has an autonomous value in Heidegger; it is to notice, rather, the way in which Lacan revises Heidegger's essay by curtailing it. Lacan's vase does not admit of an outpouring or gift; it is less like Heidegger's jug than it is like Wallace Stevens's jar, which "does not give of bird or bush, / Like nothing else in Tennessee."

This brings us next to an issue of translation. Heidegger discusses a jug (*der Krug*), which he also refers to by a more abstract term, "vessel" (*das Gefäss*). Lacan consistently uses *le vase*, which the English translation of the Seventh Seminar renders as "vase." Now *le vase* is the term by which the Gallimard translation of Heidegger (which Lacan appears to be using) renders the German *das Gefäss*, while it employs the French *la cruche* to translate *der Krug*.[13] Heidegger's choice of a "jug" imparts that bucolic homeliness which also attaches to the even more famous peasant shoes in "The Origin of the Work of Art." But Lacan's *le vase* conveys nothing of this rural charm. If Lacan uses it in the general sense of "vessel," then he is abstracting what for Heidegger is a very concrete object.

When Heidegger uses *das Gefäss,* he does so because it substantializes the *action* of holding, which he underlines through the phrase *das fassende Gefäss* ("the containing container"). Lacan's *le vase* does not do this. Moreover, *le vase,* while it can mean "vessel" in a general sense, can also mean the English "vase," as rendered by the English translation of the seminar. In this case, Lacan has constructed a far more aesthetic and less homely object that the one that Heidegger contemplates. The being of a vase, certainly, is not determined by the gift of a "gushing" or "pouring out." A vase is fully self-sufficient even when empty—perhaps *especially* when empty, if we follow Lacan's logic. The Lacanian vase is, to sum things up, a barren object when contrasted to the Heideggerian jug.

We have not done with the question of translation, however. For the French *la cruche,* which the Gallimard Heidegger uses to translate *der Krug,* also has another meaning in French popular slang: "prostitute." Now later on in the Seventh Seminar, Lacan refers approvingly to the way in which an article on sublimation by Hans Sperber establishes a relationship between the act of making a vase and "the female sexual organ" (168), and he characterizes this organ as "an opening and an emptiness" (169). One would think, then, that *la cruche* would offer the advantage of a punning reference to the "sexual symbolism" of the vase. Perhaps by not using it in the chapter "On Creation *ex nihilo,*" Lacan hopes to avoid a *premature* sexualization of the object, a reductive reading of the "emptiness" of the Thing (and of the artwork) as vaginal.[14] If this is the case, however, he has leaped out of the frying pan and into the fire, because the French *le vase* also has a sexual meaning in popular slang, where it can denote the posterior in general or the anus in particular. In *le vase,* French argot seems to keep alive the metaphorical register that allowed medieval sodomy discourse to describe the anus as a *vas* or *vasum.*

It might be argued that, where a rather abstract concept of emptiness is at stake, the distinction between anus and vagina doesn't count for much. In the Arnaut Daniel poem, it is sometimes even difficult to tell into which of the two orifices Bernart is being asked to blow. Yet I think it is fair to say that, through an accretion of small choices, Lacan privileges the anus as his paradigm for the emptiness of the Thing, and that his concept of sublimation therefore takes on a vaguely "sodomitical" cast. It is worth noting that in Heidegger's essay on "The Thing," the unifications effected by the pouring jug are described as "marriage"

(*Hochzeit*), and the unified elements are described as "betrothed" (*zuge-traut*) to one another. While Heidegger would doubtless quail at any Freudian reading of the jug, it is certainly true that the "gushing" of his Thing invokes metaphors of sexual union and fecundity, and that by contrast Lacan's vase is sterile, a mere bachelor of an object. Indeed, the pairing of sodomitical anus and decorative vase seems to land us back in the imaginary of Shakespeare's procreation sonnets, which is where this study began. Lacan's exemplary vase incorporates the specifically anal or sodomitical emptiness of the Thing, and by so doing suggests that the work of art in general is also sodomitical. We thus make one final glance, though from an even further remove, at that Pauline crux of sodomy and idolatry, art and the sublime, which I have already traced through Shakespeare, Wilde, and Freud.

A couple of caveats. First, in elucidating the anal dimensions of the Thing I do not claim to have discovered its secret. The Thing no more "is" the anus than it "is" the vagina, or the mother, or the neighbor, or Jacques Prévert's collection of empty matchboxes, or any of the other objects that come to occupy its space. The essentially veiled nature of the Thing precludes any imposing of definitional contours. All I attempt to do here is reveal the coherence of a single, overlooked facet of Lacan's discourse on the Thing, without ultimately privileging it. Lacan's anal Thing simply occupies space on the shelf with all the other Things. Second, when I speak of the anal Thing, I invoke the sodomitical anus— that is, the reconstruction of a bodily orifice by a certain discourse rather than the orifice itself.

It should nevertheless be clear by this point that Lacan's choice of poem in his "Supplementary Note" is far from random, for Lady Ena's "trumpet" retroactively highlights the anal dimensions of the vase-as-Thing. The dialectic of vacancy and fullness that Lacan locates in the latter is also played out in the former. Empty though she may be, from Lady Ena's anus "the pitch ferments upwards as it continually escapes, continually overflows." Moreover, she threatens to scald Lord Bernart's face with a stream of urine if he is foolhardy enough to obey her orders. In context, then, Lady Ena provides a rather thoroughgoing parody of Heidegger's jug, for her anal emptiness is merely prologue to the Heideggerian "gushing" which is the "outpouring of the gift"—in this case, not a libation to the gods but floods of piss and shit. Lady Ena thus reinterprets the Heideggerian gift as the Freudian gift of feces, whose sadistic charge is all too apparent. In this way she remains essentially "empty" despite her scatological overflow, thereby maintaining Lacan's revision of Heidegger's Thing.

Lacan prefaces his reference to sodomy in the *Purgatorio* by saying "I wouldn't tell all if I didn't add to the file, in case it proves useful" (*Je ne serai pas complet si je n'ajoutais au dossier, toutes fins utiles*).[15] The file, then, is not full; it contains a constitutive gap or emptiness, a *nihil* forever awaiting completion. Lacan, conversely, has not yet told all; he has not emptied himself of the remaining scholarly nuggets he holds in store. Following, as it does, hard upon his reading of the Arnaut Daniel poem, Lacan's remark seems intended to cast an ironic light on his own intellectual copiousness. Is the endless flow of his speech the divine libation of the Heideggerian jug, or the sadistic, stinking floods of Domna Ena's nether parts? Are his seminarians drinking from a holy chalice or simply blowing into the teacher's trumpet? The Thing as Lacan conceives of it is at once a vacuole and an unbearably proximate presence, emptiness and overfullness simultaneously. So, he would seem to imply, is his own sublime position as absolute master and (anal) Thing.

*   *   *

In this rendering ironic of Lacan's own position, we begin to approach the ethical dimensions of his discourse on the Thing—a difficult topic which has enjoyed deeply illuminating exegesis and development in recent years.[16] Here I want to retread some of the ground already covered by others, in order to appraise the ethical charge of the Arnaut Daniel poem with which Lacan concludes his remarks on sublimation. My comments will be oriented by two pronouncements in the Seventh Seminar: that "the question of ethics is to be articulated from the point of view of the location of man in relation to the real" (11) and that "the ethical limits of psychoanalysis coincide with the limits of its practice" (21–22). This second dictum has remained perhaps too little developed. The title *The Ethics of Psychoanalysis* refers both to the way in which psychoanalysis invents a general theory of ethics and to the fact that the analytic situation offers a privileged paradigm for ethical practice.

In elaborating the ethical dimension of Freud's work, Lacan focuses on the figure of the neighbor or *Nebenmensch* as it develops from the early *Project for a Scientific Psychology* to *Civilization and Its Discontents*.

It is in the latter work that Freud rejects the (Jewish and Christian) commandment to "love thy neighbor as thyself," finding it intolerable because
my neighbor bears cruel and destructive intentions toward me: "Man
tries to satisfy his need for aggression at the expense of his neighbor, to
exploit him without compensation, to use him sexually without his con-
sent, to appropriate his goods, to humiliate him, to inflict suffering on
him, to torture and kill him" (Lacan, 185, paraphrasing *S.E.* 21: 111). For
Lacan, the neighbor's sadistic and limitless *jouissance* marks the presence
of the Thing within him. If "to love my neighbor" means to satisfy with
my person his infinite aggression, then I am naturally hesitant to do so.
But do Christian ethics really demand so much? Isn't it really a matter of
meeting my neighbor's needs, feeding him if he is hungry and clothing
him if he is cold? For Lacan, this domesticated version of ethics counts
as doing my neighbor "good":

> My egoism is quite content with a certain altruism, altruism of the kind
> that is situated on the level of the useful. And it even becomes the pretext
> by means of which I can avoid taking up the problem of the evil I desire,
> and that my neighbor desires also. That is how I spend my life, cashing in
> my time in a dollar zone, ruble zone, or any other zone, in my neighbor's
> time, where all neighbors are maintained at the marginal level of reality of
> my own existence. (187)

This "dollar zone" is that of the pleasure principle, in which I relieve my
neighbor's suffering or *Unlust* and thus relieve my own as well. "It
is a fact of experience," notes Lacan, "that what I want is the good of
others in the image of my own. That doesn't cost so much" (187). What
does cost a great deal is to go beyond the pleasure principle and confront
my neighbor's evil, because it too is the image of my own, of the unbearable Thing I carry within me. Christianity itself shatters the barrier of its
own domesticated and neighborly "good" through the practice of those
saints and martyrs whose love for the other passes an intolerable limit:

> No doubt the question of beyond the pleasure principle, of the place of the
> unnameable Thing and of what goes on there, is raised in certain acts that
> provoke our judgment, acts of the kind attributed to a certain Angela de
> Foligino, who joyfully lapped up water in which she had just washed the
> feet of lepers—I will spare you the details, such as the fact that a piece of
> skin stuck in her throat, etc.—or to the blessed Marie Allacoque, who, with,
> no less reward in spiritual uplift, ate the excrement of a sick man. (188)

Rather than go this far, and thus confront the fact that "my neighbor's *jouissance*, his harmful, malignant *jouissance* is what poses a problem for my love" (187), it is much easier to retreat to the boundaries of the pleasure principle. But since this also betrays the real of my own desire, it results in the malaise of civilization.

For the psychoanalyst, the difficult figure of the neighbor is incarnated in the analysand or patient. Lacan asks, "Are we analysts simply something that welcomes the suppliant then, something that gives him a place of refuge? Are we simply, but it is already a lot, something that must respond to a demand, to the demand not to suffer, at least without understanding why?—in the hope that through understanding the subject will be freed not only from his ignorance, but also from suffering itself" (8). Faced with the patient as suppliant, the analyst has two choices. First, he can do the neighbor/patient "good"—that is, fulfill his demands within the limits of the pleasure principle. And the patient comes loaded with such demands—the demand to be cured, of course, or at least for the analyst to grant a meaning or explanation for suffering. And then of course there are the more local demands, for the patient wants to have his stories and his complaints validated, to have his imaginary construction of himself shored up by eliciting a sympathetic response from the analyst. A more accommodating brand of analysis than Lacan's would accede to these demands, do the patient this good, and thus try to readjust him to society's "dollar zone" of goods.

For Lacan, however, the point of analysis is to force the patient to confront the real of his desire, that is, to bring him into painful proximity with his Thing, since it is the patient's betrayal of his desire that is the ultimate source of his malaise. Not only will this confrontation prove painful for the patient, but the way to achieving it is littered with smaller cruelties, since it involves disassembling the imaginary constructs on which he has come to rely. "And in our response itself," Lacan states, "we must maintain the strictest discipline, so as not to let its deeply unconscious meaning be adulterated by that demand" (1). In practical terms, this means observing an analytical neutrality that coldly resists the patient's pleas for sympathy, love, and validation.

It is in the analytic situation that Lacan's famous articulation of Kant and Sade achieves its most striking and pertinent embodiment. For the analyst who hews rigorously to analytic technique, observing its precepts even though these cost him the pleasure of eliciting his patient's

misplaced gratitude, is the Kantian ethical subject par excellence, eschew-
ing "pathological" motives of kindness in the name of a remorseless
though ultimately therapeutic neutrality. Lacan's evocation of Kant serves
primarily to elucidate the absolute character of the *sollen* in the Freudian
apothegm "wo Es war, soll Ich werden," elaborating it into an ascetic path
for analyst and patient alike. But the very exercise of analytical neutrality
constructs a theater of cruelty for the patient, whose demands for love
are repeatedly rebuffed, whose imaginary self-construction is shattered,
and who is thereby steered toward a dreaded confrontation with the real
of his desire. Nor is it enough to say that for the patient the analyst will
falsely "appear" to be sadistic. For the fact is that the analyst has his own
Thing, and thus his own destructive *jouissance* that finds in the analytical situation a perfect apparatus and victim. One might even go so far
as to say, not that this technique is a medium for conveying sadistic
impulses but that the sadism originates and inheres in the technique
itself. "In the end, it is conceivable that it is as a pure signifying system,
as a universal maxim, as that which is most lacking in a relationship to
the individual, that the features of *das Ding* must be presented" (55).

For the analyst, as for the Sadeian hero, the exercise of destructiveness is less a source of pleasure than it is a discipline. This is the other
side of the Lacanian equation where Sade folds back into Kant. Steering
the patient toward a confrontation with the real of his desire exposes the
analyst to a kind of lethal transitivity in the Thing: "my neighbor pos-
sesses all the evil Freud speaks about, but it is no different from the evil
I retreat from in myself. To love him, to love him as myself, is necessarily to move toward some cruelty. His or mine?, you will object. But
haven't I just explained to you that nothing indicates they are distinct? It
seems rather that they are the same, on condition that these limits which
oblige me to posit myself opposite the other as fellow man are crossed"
(198). The approach to the Thing is thus not something that the analyst
can simply impose with impunity on the patient as other. Not only is the
analyst exposed to the aggressions of the patient's negative transference,
but this destructiveness is indistinguishable from that within his own
breast, and from which he "retreats," as Lacan puts it. The analyst's flight
from his own Thing is the motive of that countertransference which at
once founds the dialectic of analysis and constantly threatens to send
it off the rails. Paradoxically, the analyst is constantly "tempted by the
good," insofar as he can both defend himself from evil and earn the

temporary gratitude of the patient by abandoning the rigors of the analytical path. To remain on this path, to enforce a confrontation (his own,
the patient's) with the Thing (his patient's, his own) is the analytical
equivalent of those abject exercises undertaken by Christian saints—
the drinking of leper's water, or the ingestion of the sick man's feces.

Another, and complementary temptation arises from the problem
of *Lebensneid*, which can be defined simply as jealousy of the other's
jouissance. Since *jouissance* can never be approached directly, it can be
imagined only as a property of the other. In effect, then, *Lebensneid* is a
way of fantasizing a possible access to *jouissance*, since if others have it
then it is possible, at least in principle, that it might therefore be one's
own—though of course it never is. The patient brings his *Lebensneid*
with him as the image of the healthy and untroubled other he wishes he
could be, someone possessed of a (for the patient) unattainable vitality,
"someone who lives harmoniously and who is in any case happier than
the analysand, doesn't ask any questions and who sleeps soundly in his
bed" (237). This mirage of the healthy neighbor, the vital other, is itself a
motive for the patient's transference onto the analyst as supposedly cura-
tive agent. But on the other side, why should the analyst help another
approach a *jouissance* which he, no more than the patient, can attain?
Why not deflect the patient into the tamer zone of goods, of the good?
Here Lacan's reflections take a Nietzschean turn, exposing charitable acts
as symptoms of *ressentiment*, a kind of Christian bad faith on the part of
the analyst. The ethics of psychoanalysis thus turns traditional morality
on its head, avoiding the pleasure of the good in the name of an essentially tragic confrontation with the real of desire.

Keeping all this in mind, let us return to Arnaut Daniel's strange
little lyric. It is first of all clear that Lady Ena's test betrays a destructive
jouissance, an evil joy obtained at the expense of her lover. Her "human"
qualities are therefore extinguished in the incandescent light of the Thing
she embodies, and this is the source of her baleful sublimity. Without
constructing an absurd allegory in which the Lady would "stand in" for
either analyst or patient, we can nevertheless say that the challenge she
poses has things in common with the analytic situation. For, like psychoanalysis, she confronts the subject with the real of desire. Lady Ena does
indeed offer love, but a love beyond the pleasure principle. Unwilling to
be the imaginary mirror of male narcissism, she confronts her admirer
with something at once more vital and more terrifying, and thereby also

invites him to encounter the real of *his* desire as well. The ethical content of the Lady's challenge, if I may allow myself the liberty of translating it, would be as follows: "If, Bernart, you are afraid of the revolting pleasure of eating my shit, how can you help me on the path to my *jouissance*? How will you (filled with pity as you are) bring yourself to shit in *my* mouth, especially since I will not ask you to do it? How can I trust you not to betray your desire, to give way before it, and thus betray my desire as well?"

This challenge is harsh enough on its own, yet I perhaps simplify it by putting the words directly in Lady Ena's mouth. For the poem does not do this. Rather, it filters the Lady's demand through the dourly disapproving voice of the narrator. Her presence is thereby not only mediated but, in a sense, rendered logically impossible. For, as the narrator insists, "it is not fitting also that a lady embrace a man who has blown a stinking trumpet." The formal structure of the poem thus establishes a kind of paradox. For the purpose of the love-test is to determine whether the subject deserves access to the lady of his desire. But in this case fulfilling the test will render the subject unfit on other grounds. A kind of fold in the structure of the courtly code thus maintains the Lady in the position of impossible object. But of course this is the paradox of the Thing itself, which is at once "beyond" the symbolic network and at the same time constituted by it, so that any attempt to pass beyond the network and grasp the Thing directly causes it to disappear. It might even be argued that the poem is "about" the impossibility of sexual access. For really the Lady's test seems at one level to offer plenty. It asks: "You want to approach the impossible object of courtly desire? O.K., stick your tongue up my ass. How's that for access?" And yet, the idealized object would disappear in that moment, leaving only the emptiness of the anal Thing.

Which is also to say, the emptiness of art. Arnaut's poem reminds Lacan of the story of Pan and Syrinx as narrated by Longus:

> Pan pursues the nymph Syrinx, who runs away from him and disappears among the reeds. In his rage, he cuts down the reeds and that, Longus tells us, is the origin of the flute with pipes of unequal length—Pan wanted, the subtle poet adds, to express in that way that his love was without equal. Syrinx is transformed into the pipe of Pan's flute. Now on the level of the derision that is to be found in the strange poem that I brought to your attention here, we find the same structure, the same model of an emptiness

at the core, around which is articulated that by means of which desire is in the end sublimated. (163)

The stories are not exactly alike, of course. In Longus, the destructive rage is that of the male lover, though that too maintains the inaccessibility of the female object. Yet if the beloved remains impossibly beyond reach, that very fact, strangely enough, provides an instrument on which sexual passion can produce its music. Lacan's allusion to Syrinx reminds us that Arnaut's poem, in which the Lady asks her lover to "blow on the trumpet," also allegorizes the conversion of desire into art. Flute and trumpet are akin to the vase, not only instruments of art but images of it, in that each incorporates the void around which creation occurs.

It is right after this digression that Lacan makes his erroneous reference to Daniel and sodomy. The episode from Dante is nevertheless relevant, for in the myth of Pasiphaë and the cow built by Daedalus, sexual desire leads to the fashioning of an artifact. The wooden cow is topological cousin to the vase, another hollow invention whose rear aperture, designed for illicit sexual entry, highlights its sodomitical purpose. Significantly, the only two followers of Pasiphaë that Dante encounters and identifies are poets: Arnaut Daniel and Guido Guinizzelli, whom Dante calls "the father of me and others my betters who ever used sweet and gracious rhymes of love" (*Purg.* 26: 97–99). Punished as they are for bestial sexual excesses, Daniel and Guinizzelli bolster Lacan's point that poets do not necessarily sublimate, if this is understood to involve a desexualizing of the drives. Moreover, the placement of these poets suggests some fundamental connection between their verbal artifacts and the wooden cow of Daedalus. Both are hollow structures built to house an unspeakable *jouissance*. Lacan's error leads us, then, to a strange pinnacle which is nevertheless the proper point for a conclusion. Here on the highest rungs of Purgatory, in the subliming fires that effect a final purification, sodomites and poets trace the same circle, contrarily.

Notes

Introduction

1. Lawrence Danson, *Wilde's Intentions: The Artist in His Criticism* (New York: Oxford University Press, 1997), 106. Danson quotes Elaine Showalter, *Sexual Anarchy: Gender and Culture at the Fin de Siècle* (New York: Viking, 1990), 167.

2. Edmund Burke, *A Philosophical Enquiry into the Origins of Our Ideas of the Sublime and the Beautiful*, ed. Adam Phillips (New York: Oxford University Press, 1990).

3. Quoted in Bruce Boehrer, "Bestial Buggery in *A Midsummer Night's Dream*," in *The Production of English Renaissance Culture*, ed. David Lee Miller, Sharon O'Dair, and Harold Weber (Ithaca, N.Y.: Cornell University Press, 1994), 148.

4. G. W. F. Hegel, *Aesthetics: Lectures on Fine Art*, trans. T. M. Knox, 2 vols. (Oxford: Clarendon Press, 1975).

5. For a superb treatment of the homoerotic elements in Winkelmann's life and work, see Simon Richter, *Laocoon's Body and the Aesthetics of Pain* (Detroit: Wayne State University Press, 1992), 38–61.

6. Johann Joachim Winckelmanns *Geschichte der Kunst des Altertums* (Heidelberg: G. Weiss, 1882), 112

7. G. W. F. Hegel, *Ästhetik*, 2 vols. (Frankfurt am Main: Europäische Verlagsanstalt, 1966), 2: 126. All subsequent quotations of the German are from this edition.

Chapter 1. Shakespeare's Perfume

1. For Freud, idealization pertains to the sexual object and sublimation to the sexual aim.

2. The Willie Hughes theory is not original with Wilde. It is, in fact, an eighteenth-century invention. See Kate Chedgzoy, *Shakespeare's Queer Children: Sexual Politics and Contemporary Culture* (Manchester: Manchester University Press, 1995), 152.

3. All quotations from *The Portrait of Mr. W.H.* are taken from *The Artist*

as Critic: Critical Writings of Oscar Wilde, ed. Richard Ellman (Chicago: University of Chicago Press, 1968).

4. G. Wilson Knight, *The Mutual Flame: On Shakespeare's Sonnets and The Phoenix and the Turtle* (London: Methuen, 1955), 24–25; W. H. Auden, "Introduction" to *The Sonnets*, ed. William Burto (New York: New American Library, 1964), xxix–xxxiii; Joel Fineman, *Shakespeare's Perjured Eye: The Invention of Poetic Subjectivity in the Sonnets* (Berkeley: University of California Press, 1986), 57.

5. For an instance of this objection to sublimating readings, including Wilde's, see Joseph Pequigney, *Such Is My Love: A Study of Shakespeare's Sonnets* (Chicago: University of Chicago Press, 1985), 77–80.

6. The most resourceful and complete annotator of this wordplay is Stephen Booth in *Shakespeare's Sonnets* (New Haven, Conn.: Yale University Press, 1977). See also Pequigney, *Such Is My Love*. All quotations of the Sonnets are from Booth's edition.

7. See, e.g., Helen Vendler, *The Art of Shakespeare's Sonnets* (Cambridge, Mass.: Harvard University Press, 1997), 67. Oscar Wilde clearly sees this connection as well, but the logic of Cyril Graham's theory forces him to read the perfume bottle as a symbol of Shakespeare's dramatic, rather than lyric, art. See Wilde, *Portrait*, 173–74.

8. Compare Samuel Daniel's *Delia* II, ll. 1–4:

Goe wailing verse, the infants of my love,
Minerva-like, brought forth without a Mother:
    Present the image of the cares I prove,
Witnes your Fathers griefe exceedes all other.

Samuel Daniel, *Poems and a Defence of Ryme*, ed. Arthur Colby Sprague (Chicago: University of Chicago Press, 1965). On the sexual dynamics and figuration of male authorship, see Wayne Koestenbaum, *Double Talk: The Erotics of Male Literary Collaboration* (New York: Routledge, 1989) and Jeffrey Masten, *Textual Intercourse: Collaboration, Authorship, and Sexualities in Renaissance Drama* (New York: Cambridge University Press, 1997).

9. Nicolas Flamel, *Nicholas Flamel: His Exposition of the Hieroglyphicall figures ... Together with The secret Booke of ARTEPHIUS* (London, 1624), ed. Laurinda Dixon (New York: Garland, 1994), 67.

10. Flamel, *Nicholas Flamel*, 77–78: "And so in such a regiment the *Body* is made a *spirit* of a subtile nature, and the *spirit* is incorporated with the *Body*, and is made one with it, and in such a sublimation, conjunction, and elevation, all things are made *white*."

11. Flamel, 76–77: "It behooveth therefore that (as Sibill said) *the Sonne of the Virgin bee exalted from the Earth*, and that the white *quintessence* after his resurrection bee lifted up towards the heavens."

12. Flamel, 30.

13. Flamel, 73. Compare George Ripley, "The Mistery of Alchymists," in Elias Ashmole, *Theatricum Chemicum Britannicum* (London, 1652), ed. Allen G. Debus (New York: Johnson Reprint, 1967), 385:

> For whereas Woman is in presence,
> There is much moysture and accidence,
> Wetnes and humours in her be,
> The which would drown'd our Quality;
> Perceive well (*son*) by *Noah's* flood,
> To much moysture was never good

14. John Donne, *The Complete English Poems*, ed. A. J. Smith (New York: Penguin, 1971).

15. This second movement emerges if the "we" of the poem's antepenultimate line is read as referring, not to Donne and his mistress, but to Donne and the male friend.

16. See Sonnet 114. See also the comments on Sonnets 20 and 33 in Raymond B. Waddington, "The Poetics of Eroticism: Shakespeare's 'Master-Mistress,'" in *Renaissance Discourses of Desire*, ed. Claude J. Summers and Ted-Larry Pebworth (Columbia: University of Missouri Press, 1993), 15–16.

17. For an extended analysis of these qualities, though not in an alchemical context, see Margreta De Grazia's stimulating essay, "The Scandal of Shakespeare's Sonnets," *Shakespeare Survey* 46 (1993): 35–49.

18. In *A Midsummer Night's Dream*, Theseus counsels Hermia that if she disobeys her father's commandment to marry Demetrius she must either die or become a nun. He praises a life of virginity, then adds:

> But earthlier happy is the rose distill'd,
> Than that which withering on the virgin thorn
> Grows, lives, and dies in single blessedness. (1.1.76–78)

Theseus's image of female *jouissance* is, of course, suffused with his own phallic sadism. The best gloss on his lines may be provided by Emily Dickinson:

> Essential Oils are wrung—
> The attar from the Rose
> Is not expressed by Suns—alone—
> It is the gift of Screws—

The Poems of Emily Dickinson: Variorum Edition, ed. R.W. Franklin (Cambridge, Mass.: Harvard University Press, 1998), 2: 728.

19. Pequigney, *Such Is My Love*, 12. Sonnet 13 might seem to offer a partial exception, since the second quatrain does argue for the maintenance of a home:

> Who lets so fair a house fall to decay,
> Which husbandry in honour might uphold
> Against the stormy gust of winter's day
> And barren rage of death's eternal cold? (9–13)

Even here, however, Shakespeare emphasizes the physically protective qualities of the house, not its status as patrimony. Indeed, nothing in these lines specifies that the house is inherited. Moreover, the argument is purely metaphorical, since the house as property stands for the young man's "beauty which you hold in lease" (5). The sonnet, therefore, does not argue *directly*, and perhaps not even indirectly, that the young man should reproduce in order to perpetuate a noble house.

20. Shakespeare's arguments for procreation portray it as something desirable, prudent, perhaps approaching an obligation, but still not a law or commandment as these would be understood in either a juridical or theological sense. That is to say, the sonnets stop short of issuing an absolute *injunction* to reproduce. Nothing like the Judeo-Christian God stands ready to punish the failure to do so. Which is not to say that personified forces aren't at work here. But they manage to sidestep the realm of divine commandment. The first of these forces is, of course, Time, whose baleful presence pervades the whole sequence. Variously described as a "bloody tyrant" (16: 2), "devouring" (19: 1), "wasteful" (11: 11), Time is the relentless destroyer of youth and beauty. Time does indeed enforce something like an absolute and unavoidable "law." Yet age is never described as a consequence of sin or crime or humanity's fallen nature. It is simply pure inexorability without motive. Time, that is, exacts something like punishment, but emptied of purpose—the form of divine justice without its content, a metaphysically abstract sadism.

The second of Shakespeare's personifications, Nature, is portrayed as a bounteous, beneficent mother who counsels childbearing as a way of evading Time's otherwise inexorable doom. Nature's generosity does not demand procreation but seems merely to expect a kind of counter-generosity on the part of her creatures. See Sonnet 11: 11–14 and Sonnet 4: 3–4. But this expectation can neither demand the fact nor specify the terms of counter-generosity, since that would violate the very freedom that is the basis of the gift. Nature, therefore, does not punish those who violate her wishes; she is, at worst, disapproving. To be a "niggard" or "usurer" (4: 5, 7) is simply to act in an unseemly or ignoble fashion in the face of Nature's bounty. It violates an *aesthetics* of behavior, resulting in shame but not punishment.

The exhortation to procreate thus obeys "beauty's law" in two senses, for the obligation to create beauty is regulated or enforced only by the norms of beauty. The procreation sonnets never suggest that the failure to reproduce is a sin. They simply portray it as foolish and selfish—ignoble and unattractive behavior.

21. Mark Jordan, *The Invention of Sodomy in Christian Theology* (Chicago: University of Chicago Press, 1997), 158.

22. See Jordan, *Invention of Sodomy*, 143, 156.

23. "The Tears of an Affectionate Shepheard Sicke for Love," 95–102. Quoted from Richard Barnfield, *The Complete Poems*, ed. George Klawitter (Selinsgrove, Pa.: Susquehanna University Press, 1990).

24. For a suggestive treatment of Lot's wife and the problem of the spectator, see Martin Harries, "Forgetting Lot's Wife: Artaud, Spectatorship, and Catastrophe," *Yale Journal of Criticism* 11, 1 (1998): 221–38.

25. Peter Damian, *Book of Gomorrah: An Eleventh-Century Treatise Against Clerical Homosexual Practices*, trans. Pierre J. Payer (Waterloo, Ont.: Wilfrid Laurier University Press, 1982).

26. See Jordan, *Invention of Sodomy*, 29.

27. For a secularized version of this thesis see Jacques Chiffoleau, "Dire l'indicible: Remarques sur la catégorie du *nefandum* du XIIe au Xve siècle," *Annales* 45 (1990): 289–324. Chiffoleau situates the dangerous silence surrounding the *nefandum* with the respectable one surrounding political Majesty. See esp. 294.

28. John Bale, *The Complete Plays of John Bale*, ed. Peter Happé, vol. 2 (Cambridge: D.S. Brewer, 1986).

29. Although I am here pursuing the connection between sodomy and sublimity in a Judeo-Christian context, the figure of Ganymede provides an important analogue in classical culture. See Leonard Barkan, *Transuming Passion: Ganymede and the Erotics of Humanism* (Stanford, Calif.: Stanford University Press, 1991). It is noteworthy that Shakespeare's sonnets not only fail to cite Ganymede but display unusual restraint compared to other contemporary sonnet sequences in their use of all classical allusion.

30. See George Economou, *The Goddess Natura in Medieval Literature* (Cambridge, Mass.: Harvard University Press, 1972).

31. See Economou, *Goddess Natura*, 55.

32. Quoted in Economou, *Goddess Natura*, 100.

33. Compare Richard Barnfield's sonnets 9 and 10, in which Venus (called "Creatrix" in sonnet 10) fashions Ganymede from a mixture of snow and Diana's blood.

34. On rabbinical exegetes, see Daniel Boyarin, *Carnal Israel: Reading Sex in Talmudic Culture* (Berkeley: University of California Press, 1993), 35–46. On Renaissance Platonists, see Edgar Wind, *Pagan Mysteries in the Renaissance*, rev. ed. (New York: Norton, 1968), 212–14.

35. Things are more complicated than this, however. The addition of the penis may raise the specter of sodomy for the speaker, but it avoids it for Nature herself, who had begun dangerously to "dote" on this proto-female.

36. Slavoj Žižek, *The Metastases of Enjoyment: Six Essays on Woman and Causality* (New York: Verso, 1994), 103.

37. Jonathan Goldberg, "*Romeo and Juliet's* Open Rs," in *Queering the Renaissance*, ed. Goldberg (Durham, N.C.: Duke University Press, 1994), 225.

38. Marquis de Sade, *The 120 Days of Sodom, and Other Writings*, trans. Austryn Wainhouse and Richard Seaver (New York: Grove Press, 1966), 197.

39. Sade, *120 Days*, 233.

40. Sade, *120 Days*, 234.

41. On violence and the Renaissance blazon, see Nancy Vickers, "'The blazon of sweet beauty's best': Shakespeare's *Lucrece*," in *Shakespeare and the Question of Theory*, ed Patricia Parker and Geoffrey Hartman (New York: Methuen, 1985), 95–115, as well as Vickers, "Diana Described: Scattered Women and Scattered Rhyme," in *Writing and Sexual Difference*, ed. Elizabeth Abel (New York: Routledge, 1982), 99–109.

Chapter 2. Theory to Die For

1. See, e.g., Michael Bérubé, *The Employment of English: Theory, Jobs, and the Future of Literary Studies* (New York: New York University Press, 1998).

2. It is important to recognize that every theoretical framework serves not only as a means of producing new knowledge and insight but also as a way of screening out a potentially overwhelming set of data by deciding which will or will not count as information. Theory thus works like that baked-through outer layer on the fictional animalcule that Freud imagines in chapter 4 of *Beyond the Pleasure Principle*. By filtering and binding energies, theory serves to maintain the internal homeostasis that, in Freud's view, is allied with the death-drive.

3. Kate Chedgzoy, *Shakespeare's Queer Children: Sexual Politics and Contemporary Culture* (Manchester: Manchester University Press, 1995), 144.

4. This was the original version of the story. My essay quotes from the later elaboration of the story that was first published posthumously, in 1921.

5. H. Montgomery Hyde, *The Trials of Oscar Wilde* (New York: Dover, 1962), 124. Wilde is here responding to the charge that *Dorian Gray* is "open to the interpretation" of being a "perverted novel."

6. John Guillory, *Cultural Capital: The Problem of Literary Canon Formation* (Chicago: University of Chicago Press, 1993), 181–207.

7. William A. Cohen, "Willie and Wilde: Reading *The Portrait of Mr. W.H.*" *South Atlantic Quarterly* 88, 1 (Winter 1989): 219–45; quotation from 229.

8. Slavoj Žižek, *The Sublime Object of Ideology* (New York: Verso, 1989), 105.

9. Wilde stated in a letter to Louis Wilkinson that he did believe in the theory. On the letter, on the question of Wilde's belief, on whether early reviewers believed that he believed in the theory, and on the status of truth in the *Portrait*, see Kevin Kopelson, "Wilde, Barthes, and the Orgasmics of Truth," *Genders* 7 (1990): 22–31.

10. Ignatius Donnelly, *The Great Cryptogam: Francis Bacon's Cipher in the So-Called Shakespeare Plays* (1887; reprint New York: AMS, 1972).

11. Martin Ridge, *Ignatius Donnelly: The Portrait of a Politician* (Chicago: University of Chicago Press, 1962), 238.

12. But as Richard Ellman notes in his biography *Oscar Wilde* (New York:

Vintage, 1988), the *Portrait* "was being written ... by October 1887" (291). Hence Donnelly's lecture could not have originated the idea for the story. At most it deepened a theme on which Wilde was already at work.

13. Wilde observes more generally that "It is through its incompleteness that Art becomes complete in beauty" (370).

14. See Žižek, *Sublime Object*, 123.

15. "[A]s art springs from personality, so it is only to personality that it can be revealed, and from the meeting of the two comes right interpretive criticism" (374).

16. Joel Fineman, *Shakespeare's Perjured Eye*, 29.

17. The narrator describes one of Shakespeare's sonnets to Willie as expressing "mad idolatry" (179).

18. See Linda Dowling, *Hellenism and Homosexuality in Victorian Oxford* (Ithaca, N.Y.: Cornell University Press, 1994), 142–43.

19. Michel Foucault, *Madness and Civilization: A History of Insanity in the Age of Reason,* trans. Richard Howard (New York: Vintage, 1988).

20. In *Madness and Civilization* Foucault develops the themes of sublimity less fully with respect to madness itself than with respect to the figure of the psychoanalyst, who both dispels and concentrates the institutional powers of the asylum. Freud, he claims, "amplified" the "thaumaturgical virtues" of the clinic and concentrated them on the person of the analyst. "He focussed upon this single presence—concealed behind the patient and above him, in an absence that is also a total presence—all the powers that had been distributed in the collective existence of the asylum; he transformed this into an absolute Observation, a pure and circumspect Silence, a Judge who punishes and rewards in a judgment that does not even condescend to language" (277–78). In *The Order of Things*, psychoanalysis is granted a more heroic and less repressive, though no less sublime role as one of two discourses (along with ethnology) that explore the limits of human finitude. Psychoanalysis "leaps over representation, overflows it on the side of finitude"; it "frames and defines, on the outside, the very possibility of representation" (Michel Foucault, *The Order of Things: An Archeology of the Human Sciences* [New York: Random House, 1973], 374, 375). Psychoanalysis is now portrayed less as the antagonist than as the double or ally of both madness and of modern literary figures such as Artaud (383). This relation between analyst and patient revises, but does not reverse the one portrayed in *Madness and Civilization*, where the analyst is already both antagonist and double of the madman.

21. The essay, first given as a lecture in 1963 and then published in *Revue de métaphysique et de morale* (1964), was later included in Derrida's volume *Writing and Difference* (1967); trans. Alan Bass (Chicago: University of Chicago Press, 1978), 31–63.

22. Derrida's endnote 9 (308) directs us to the relevant passages without comment. In *The Post Card*, a later work, Derrida will become more explicit about the erotic dimensions of Socratic *hubris* and pedagogy. Describing a thirteenth-century illustration depicting Plato and Socrates, he writes: "I see

Plato getting an erection in *Socrates'* back and see the insane hubris of his prick, an interminable, disproportionate erection ... slowly sliding, still warm, under *Socrates'* right leg." (Jacques Derrida, *The Post Card: From Socrates to Freud and Beyond,* trans. Alan Bass [Chicago: University of Chicago Press, 1987], 18). But here, in the earlier context of the debate with Foucault, Derrida's allusion is relatively muted. Lee Edelman comments on the passage from *The Post Card* in *Homographesis: Essays in Gay Literary and Cultural Theory* (New York: Routledge, 1994), 188–91.

23. On the influence of Greek pederasty and Socratic eros on Wilde and Victorian culture generally, see Dowling, chapters 3 and 4.

24. Michel Foucault, "My Body, This Paper, This Fire," trans. Geoff Bennington, *Oxford Literary Review* 4 (1979): 9–28.

25. Jacques Derrida, *Résistances de la psychanalyse* (Paris: Galilée, 1996); *Resistances of Psychoanalysis,* trans. Peggy Kamuf, Pascale-Anne Brault, and Michael Naas (Stanford, Calif.: Stanford University Press, 1998).

26. Derrida, *Résistances de la psychanalyse,* 93; English ed. 70.

27. On the "enemy-friend," see Jacques Derrida, *Politics of Friendship,* trans. George Collins (New York: Verso), 1997.

Chapter 3. Freud's Egyptian Renaissance

1. In a letter to Sándor Ferenczi, Freud writes: "Don't be concerned about the Leonardo. I have long written only for the small circle which every day widens, and if the other people didn't rail about the Leonardo I should have gone astray in my opinion of them." Quoted in Ernest Jones, *The Life and Work of Sigmund Freud,* 3 vols. (New York: Basic Books, 1953–57), 2: 347.

2. All English quotations of this work come from volume 11 of *The Standard Edition of the Complete Psychological Works of Sigmund Freud,* ed. James Strachey et al., 24 vols. (London: Hogarth Press, 1953–74). When citing volume 11 in this chapter I give only page numbers. Citations from other volumes use the abbreviation *S.E.* with volume and page numbers. Quotations of the German text come from the *Gesammelte Werke, chronologische geordnet,* ed. Anna Freud, 17 vols. (London: Imago, 1940–52), abbreviated *G.W.*

3. "Freud ... destroys the artist as idol in practice, if not in what he says." Sarah Kofman, *The Childhood of Art: An Interpretation of Freud's Aesthetics,* trans. Winifred Woodhull (New York: Columbia University Press, 1988), 15. See chapter 1 of Kofman's book for a discussion of Freud's artistic iconoclasm and his identification with Moses.

4. As Bradley I. Collins notes, "the charge of sodomy brought against Leonardo remains equivocal." See Collins, *Leonardo, Psychoanalysis, and Art History: A Critical Study of Psychobiographical Approaches to Leonardo da Vinci* (Evanston, Ill.: Northwestern University Press, 1997), 80. For a recent scholarly treatment of Leonardo's sexuality, see Carlo Pedretti, "The Angel in the Flesh," *Achademia Leonardi Vinci: Journal of Leonardo Studies* 4 (1991): 34–51.

5. The Standard Edition gives "invert" for "homosexual." The latter appears only in the original 1910 edition.

6. The most extended and influential critique of Freud's book is an essay by Meyer Schapiro, "Leonardo and Freud: An Art-Historical Study," *Journal of the History of Ideas* 17, 2 (1956): 147–78. In response to Schapiro's essay, the psychoanalyst Kurt Eissler wrote a book-length defense and expansion of Freud's ideas about Leonardo. See K. R. Eissler, *Leonardo da Vinci: Psychoanalytic Notes on the Enigma* (London: Hogarth Press, 1962). For an assessment of this debate in light of contemporary evidence and an attempt at balancing the disciplinary claims of psychoanalysis and art history, see Collins, *Leonardo*. Juliana Schiesari, "Mothers of Invention: Rereading Freud and Leonardo," in *Repossessions: Psychoanalysis and the Phantasms of Early Modern Culture*, ed. Timothy Murray and Alan K. Smith (Minneapolis: University of Minnesota Press, 1998), 200–220 also attempts to criticize Freud's account, in part by drawing on evidence from Leonardo's notebooks.

7. I am using this term in a way that is vaguely related to the concept of encryption as elaborated by Nicholas Abraham and Maria Torok. See their book *The Wolf Man's Magic Word: A Cryptonomy*, trans. Nicholas Rand (Minneapolis: University of Minnesota Press, 1986).

8. Some of these complications will be addressed in this chapter's third section. Here I might note that, while Freud posits Leonardo's identification with the Christ child (90), Leonardo's own maternal impulses, as exhibited toward his pupils, allows a reading of the *St. Anne with Two Others* in which he identifies with the two mother-figures as well.

9. Freud, it should be said, does not use the word "trauma" anywhere in his Leonardo book. But it is strongly implicit in his analysis, and it forms an important element in the work of later writers, especially Eissler, who argues that "Leonardo was excessively vulnerable to traumata" (*Leonardo*, 13). But Eissler sees the fundamental trauma in Leonardo's life as the separation from his mother, rather than his mother's excessive sexual demand. On trauma and sublimation more generally, with some reference to Freud's Leonardo book, see Jean Laplanche, *Problématiques III: La Sublimation* (Paris: Presses Universitaires de France, 1980), 215–71.

10. G. W. F. Hegel, *Ästhetik*, 2 vols. (Frankfurt am Main: Europäische Verlagsanstalt, 1966); *Aesthetics: Lectures on Fine Art*, trans. T. M. Knox, 2 vols. (Oxford: Clarendon Press, 1975).

11. I recognize, of course, that when Freud wrote his Leonardo book he had not yet evolved the later topography of id-ego-superego. But this topography seems to me to manifest itself in an unmistakable though still latent form.

12. Eric Maclagan, "Leonardo in the Consulting Room," *Burlington Magazine* 42 (January 1923): 51–54, first notes the error. For an account of its transmission by later writers, see Richard Wohl and Harry Trosman, "A Retrospect of Freud's *Leonardo*," *Psychiatry* 18 (February 1955): 27–39, esp. 32–33. Schapiro makes use of the error in his more thoroughgoing critique of Freud's essay. For a recent discussion, see Alan Bass, "On the History of a Mistranslation and the

Psychoanalytic Movement," in *Difference in Translation*, ed. Joseph F. Graham (Ithaca, N.Y.: Cornell University Press, 1985), 102–41.

13. But in one of those strange accidents that occur so often in Freud, legend holds that the hawk (of which Leonardo's *nibbio* is a variety), like the vulture, was also of one gender—female. See Wayne Anderson, "Leonardo da Vinci and the Slip of Fools," *History of European Ideas* 18, 1 (1994): 63.

14. First pointed out by Ernest Jones, the identification extends from Leonardo's sexual disposition to the battle within him between the scientist and the artist. See Jones, *Life*, 2: 346.

15. The connection is made, for instance, by Eva M. Rosenfeld, "Dream and Vision: Some Remarks on Freud's Egyptian Bird Dream," *International Journal of Psychoanalysis* 37 (1956): 98 and by Ilse Barande, *Le Maternel singulier: Freud et Léonard da Vinci* (Paris: Aubier Montaigne, 1977), 107–8.

16. Similarly, the phrase translated as "my beloved mother" in the Standard Edition is actually "die geliebte Mutter" (*G.W.* 2/3: 589), "*the* beloved mother."

17. Freud's description of the young man as "der welterfahrenden Lehrmeister" (*G.W.* 2/3: 589) is a bit of drollery whose deprecating humor might well be a defensive reaction.

18. For a discussion, see Rosenfeld, "Dream and Vision."

19. Yosef Hayim Yerushalmi, *Freud's Moses: Judaism Terminable and Interminable* (New Haven, Conn.: Yale University Press, 1991), 71.

20. Yerushalmi, *Freud's Moses*, 73–74

21. On Freud's collection of antiquities, see Lynn Garnwell and Richard Wells, eds., *Sigmund Freud and Art: His Personal Collection of Antiquities* (New York: Harry Abrams, 1989), and Stephen Barker, ed., *Excavations and Their Objects; Freud's Collection of Antiquity* (Albany: State University of New York Press, 1996).

22. Cf. Gérard Huber, *L'Égypte ancienne dans la psychanalyse* (Paris: Masionneuve et Larose, 1987), 125.

23. Huber, *L'Égypte ancienne*, 127.

24. It is a nice irony that Freud's (originally anonymous) essay on Michelangelo first appeared in the journal named *Imago*.

25. Huber, *L'Égypte ancienne*, 50, 58.

26. Like the theme of idolatry, that of homosexuality takes on autobiographical dimensions for Freud. In a letter to Sándor Ferenczi dated October 17, 1910 (about six months after the completion of the Leonardo book), Freud announces "the overcoming of my homosexuality, with the result being greater independence" (*The Correspondence of Sigmund Freud and Sándor Ferenczi*, ed. Eva Brabant et al., 2 vols. (Cambridge, Mass.: Harvard University Press, 1993–96), 2: 227. Freud provides a gloss on this puzzling announcement when he writes, on December 16 of that year, "I have now overcome Fliess, which you were so curious about" (2: 243). Jeffrey Moussaieff Masson links these two letters in *The Assault on Truth: Freud's Suppression of the Seduction Theory* (New York: Farrar, Straus and Giroux, 1984), 207–8, n. 15. By his "homosexuality,"

Freud thus apparently means his formative and vexed relationship with Wilhelm Fliess. Like Leonardo's, Freud's "homosexuality" was apparently "ideal" or sublimated, taking the form of an excessive attachment to Fliess's person and his peculiar medical theories. It was from Fliess, in fact, that Freud seems to have borrowed the postulate of originary bisexuality; and a dispute over priority in this matter was a triggering event in Freud's break with Fliess (see Jones, *Life*, 2: 214–18).

Freud's Leonardo book has everything to do with his relationship to Fliess. To take one example: in the 1890s Fliess had elaborated a theory connecting left-handedness with bisexuality, and in this context he suggested that Freud himself was left-handed, a suggestion that Freud jokingly rebuffed. Freud, in fact, initially rejected Fliess's theory of bilaterality and bisexuality, though by 1901 he wrote to Fliess that he is now testing his patients for left-handedness. See *The Complete Letters of Sigmund Freud to Wilhelm Fliess, 1887–1904*, ed. and trans Jeffrey Moussaieff Masson (Cambridge, Mass.: Harvard University Press, 1985), 292–94, 436. Moreover, on October 9, 1898, Freud wrote to Fliess: "Leonardo—no love affair of his is known—is perhaps the most famous left-handed person. Can you use him?" (331).

Years later, while Freud was at work on the Leonardo book, Ernest Jones remarked in a letter: "You know it has recently been proved he [Leonardo] was not left-handed," to which Freud responded: "I think he was 'bimanual,' but that is about the same thing as left-handed. I have not inquired further into his hand writing, because I avoided by purpose all biological view [sic] restraining myself to the discussion of the psychological ones" (*The Complete Correspondence of Sigmund Freud and Ernest Jones, 1908–1939*, ed. R. Andrew Paskauskas [Cambridge, Mass.: Harvard University Press, 1993], 49, 51). What Freud is "avoiding" here is Fliess, whose theory of bisexuality was precisely biological—indeed, cellular. By propounding a purely psychological analysis of Leonardo's homosexuality, Freud detaches himself from Fliess's biological speculation, repudiates Fliess's priority on the question of originary bisexuality (since Freud's understanding of this concept now owes nothing to Fliess), and, in a more general way, frees himself from Fliess's residual influence. This is what Freud means when he speaks of "overcoming" Fliess and of gaining greater intellectual independence thereby. Ironically, then, Freud's most extended essay on homosexuality was, for him, a way of "overcoming" his most intellectually formative same-sex attachment.

27. See Kofman, *The Childhood of Art*, chap. 3: "Freud's Method of Reading: The Work of Art as a Text to Decipher."

28. In the Leonardo book, Freud describes Pfister's discovery as being "of undeniable interest, even if one may not feel inclined to accept it without reserve" (115n). In correspondence with Ferenczi, Freud writes: "Our colleagues seem to like Leonardo. Pfister has become a visionary through him and sees the outline of a vulture in the white cloth around the body of Mary." Yet, he adds, this reading "seems possible to me." *Correspondence of Freud and Ferenczi*, 1: 180.

29. Oscar Pfister, "Kryptolalie, Kryptographie und unbewusstes Vexier-bild bei Normalen," *Jahrbuch für Psychoanalytische und Psychopathologische Forschungen* 5 (1913): 117–56.

30. Alan Bass ("On the History of a Mistranslation," 137) makes a suggestive analogy between Pfister's seeing what is not there (the vulture), and the child's "seeing" the maternal phallus, which results in fetishism.

31. Jean Laplanche, *Problématiques III*, 17.

32. On Freud's vexed and contradictory attempt to distinguish sublimation from the return of the repressed, see, e.g., Laplanche, *Problématiques III*, 33, and Collins, *Leonardo*, 8.

33. Collins, *Leonardo*, 11–12.

34. Barande, *La Maternel singulier*, 63. Barande also reads Leonardo's painting as a maternalization of Genesis.

Chapter 4. Lacan's Anal Thing

1. Jacques Lacan, *The Ethics of Psychoanalysis, 1959–1960*, trans. Dennis Porter (New York: Norton, 1992).

2. Although he does not cite it, Lacan quotes the prose translation in *Les Poésies d'Arnaut Daniel*, trans and commentary René Lavaud (Toulouse: Eduoard Privat, 1910), 6–11.

3. For a discussion of this chapter from a slightly different perspective, see Slavoj Žižek, "Courtly Love, or Woman as Thing," in Žižek, *The Metastases of Enjoyment: Six Essays on Woman and Causality* (New York: Verso, 1994), 89–112.

4. Sodomites do appear in Cantos XV and XVI of the *Inferno*, however. Lacan's "XIV" probably results from unconsciously transposing the numbers of *Inferno* "XVI" and transferring them to the *Purgatorio*.

5. Dante Alighieri, *The Divine Comedy*, trans. and commentary Charles Singleton (Princeton, N.J.: Princeton University Press, 1970).

6. Lacan addresses this prohibition more directly on p. 196.

7. For more on Lacan's vase and Heidegger's Thing, see Julia Reinhard Lupton and Kenneth Reinhard, *After Oedipus: Shakespeare in Psychoanalysis* (Ithaca, N.Y.: Cornell University Press, 1993), 178–89; see also Christopher Fynsk, "Between Ethics and Creation," *L'Esprit Créateur* 35, 3 (1995): 80–87.

8. In his seminar on "The Purloined Letter," Lacan uses the example of the catalogue numbering system in a library to show how only a symbolic system can create absence: "what is hidden is never but what is *missing from its place*, as the call slip puts it when speaking of a volume that is lost from the library. And even if the book be on the adjacent shelf or in the next slot, it would be hidden there, however visibly it may appear. For it can *literally* be said that something is missing from its place only of what can change it: the symbolic. For the real, whatever upheaval we subject it to, is always in its place; it carries it glued to its heel, ignorant of what might exile it from it."

Jacques Lacan, "Seminar on 'The Purloined Letter,'" trans. Jeffrey Mehlman, in *The Purloined Poe: Lacan, Derrida, and Psychoanalytic Reading*, ed. John P. Muller and William J. Richardson (Baltimore: Johns Hopkins University Press, 1988), 40.

9. *The Complete Poetry and Prose of William Blake*, newly rev. ed., ed. David Erdman (Berkeley: University of California Press, 1982), 39.

10. See W. T. J. Mitchell, *Blake's Composite Art: A Study of the Illuminated Poetry* (Princeton, N.J.: Princeton University Press, 1978), 41, and Northrop Frye, *Fearful Symmetry: A Study of William Blake* (Princeton, N.J.: Princeton University Press, 1947), 200.

11. This information comes from an email communication with Mark Jordan.

12. Martin Heidegger, *Poetry, Language, Thought* (New York: Harper and Row, 1971), 169; German from Heidegger, *Vorträge und Aufsätze* (Pfullingen: Neskein, 1954), 41.

13. Martin Heidegger, *Essais et conférences*, trans. André Préau (Paris: Gallimard, 1958).

14. Of course French *chose*, like German *Ding* and English "thing," can refer to the genitals of either sex. But *chose* is a euphemism that can replace any number of "naughty" words. *Harrap's Slang*, for instance, gives "Je vais te botter le chose" or "I'll kick you up the you-know-what"—presumably, the ass. *Harrap's Slang Dictionary/Dictionnaire* (Edinburgh and Paris: Harrap, 1993). When Lacan plays on the word *chose* in his discussion of Lady Ena's "thing," the word seems indeterminate in its meaning. *Le Robert* says of *chose*: "Substituable à n'importe quel autre nom que l'on ne peut se rappeller, ou dont on veut éviter l'emploi." *Le Grand Robert de la langue Française*, 2nd ed. (Paris: Le Robert, 1985), 2: 592. The euphemistic character of the word suggests something that is orbited by the signifier.

15. *Le Séminaire de Jacques Lacan*, vol. 7, *L'Éthique de la psychanalyse, 1959–1960*, ed. Jacques-Alain Miller (Paris: Éditions du Seuil, 1986), 194.

16. I am thinking here of John Rachjman's "Lacan and the Ethics of Modernity," *Representations* 15 (Summer 1986): 42–56 and two equally fine essays by Kenneth Reinhard, "Freud, my Neighbor," *American Imago* 54, 2 (Summer 1997): 165–95 and "Kant with Sade, Lacan with Levinas," *MLN* 110, 4 (September 1995): 785–808. I happily acknowledge my indebtedness to all three of these.

Bibliography

Abraham, Nicholas and Maria Torok. *The Wolf Man's Magic Word: A Cryptonomy.* Trans. Nicholas Rand. Minneapolis: University of Minnesota Press, 1986.

Anderson, Wayne. "Leonardo da Vinci and the Slip of Fools." *History of European Ideas* 18, 1 (1994): 61–78.

Arnaut Daniel. *Les Poésies d'Arnaut Daniel.* Trans. with commentary René Lavaud. Toulouse: Eduoard Privat, 1910.

Ashmole, Elias. *Theatricum Chemicum Britannicum.* London, 1652. Reprint New York: Johnson Reprints, 1967.

Auden, W. H. Introduction to William Shakespeare, *The Sonnets,* ed. William Burto, xvii–xxxviii. New York: New American Library, 1964.

Bale, John. *The Complete Plays of John Bale.* Ed. Peter Hupp. Cambridge: D.S. Brewer, 1986.

Barande, Ilse. *Le Maternel singulier: Freud et Léonard da Vinci.* Paris: Aubier Montaigne, 1977.

Barkan, Leonard. *Transuming Passion: Ganymede and the Erotics of Humanism.* Stanford, Calif.: Stanford University Press, 1991.

Barker, Stephen, ed. *Excavations and Their Objects: Freud's Collection of Antiquity.* Albany: State University of New York Press, 1996.

Barnfield, Richard. *The Complete Poems.* Ed. George Klawitter. Selinsgrove, Pa.: Susquehanna University Press, 1990.

Bass, Alan. "On the History of a Mistranslation and the Psychoanalytic Movement." In *Difference in Translation,* ed. Joseph F. Graham, 102–41. Ithaca, N.Y.: Cornell University Press, 1985.

Blake, William. *The Complete Poetry and Prose of William Blake.* Newly revised ed. Ed. David Erdman. Berkeley: University of California Press, 1982.

Boehrer, Bruce. "Bestial Buggery in *A Midsummer Night's Dream.*" In *The Production of English Renaissance Culture,* ed. David Lee Miller, Sharon O'Dair, and Harold Weber, 123–50. Ithaca, N.Y.: Cornell University Press, 1994.

Boyarin, Daniel. *Carnal Israel: Reading Sex in Talmudic Culture.* Berkeley: University of California Press, 1993.

Bérubé, Michael. *The Employment of English: Theory, Jobs, and the Future of Literary Studies.* New York: New York University Press, 1998.

Burke, Edmund. *A Philosophical Enquiry into the Origins of our Ideas of the*

Sublime and the Beautiful. Ed. Adam Phillips. New York: Oxford University Press, 1990.

Chedgzoy, Kate. *Shakespeare's Queer Children: Sexual Politics and Contemporary Culture.* Manchester: Manchester University Press, 1995.

Chiffoleau, Jacques. "Dire l'indicible. Remarques sur la catégorie du *nefandum* du XIIe au Xve siècle." *Annales* 45 (1990): 289–324.

Cohen, William A. "Willie and Wilde: Reading *The Portrait of Mr. W.H.*." *South Atlantic Quarterly* 88, 1 (Winter 1989): 219–45.

Collins, Bradley I. *Leonardo, Psychoanalysis, and Art History: A Critical Study of Psychobiographical Approaches to Leonardo da Vinci.* Evanston, Ill.: Northwestern University Press, 1997.

Damian, Peter. *Book of Gomorrah: An Eleventh-Century Treatise Against Clerical Homosexual Practices.* Trans. Pierre J. Payer. Waterloo, Ont.: Wilfrid Laurier University Press, 1982.

Daniel, Samuel. *Poems and a Defence of Ryme.* Ed. Arthur Colby Sprague. Chicago: University of Chicago Press, 1965.

Danson, Lawrence. *Wilde's Intentions: The Artist in His Criticism.* New York: Oxford University Press, 1997.

Dante Alighieri. *The Divine Comedy.* Trans. with commentary Charles Singleton. Princeton, N.J.: Princeton University Press, 1970.

De Grazia, Margreta. "The Scandal of Shakespeare's Sonnets." *Shakespeare Survey* 46 (1993): 35–49.

Derrida, Jacques. *Politics of Friendship.* Trans. George Collins. New York: Verso, 1997.

_____. *The Post Card: From Socrates to Freud and Beyond.* Trans. Alan Bass. Chicago: University of Chicago Press, 1987.

_____. *Résistances de la psychanalyse.* Paris: Éditions Galilée, 1996.

_____. *Resistances of Psychoanalysis.* Trans. Peggy Kamuf, Pascale-Anne Brault, and Michael Naas. Stanford, Calif.: Stanford University Press, 1998.

_____. *Writing and Difference.* Trans. Alan Bass. Chicago: University of Chicago Press, 1978.

Dickinson, Emily. *The Poems of Emily Dickinson: Variorum Edition.* Ed. R. W. Franklin. 3 vols. Cambridge, Mass.: Belknap Press of Harvard University Press, 1998.

Donne, John. *The Complete English Poems.* Ed. A. J. Smith. New York: Penguin, 1971.

Donnelly, Ignatius. *The Great Cryptogram: Francis Bacon's Cipher in the So-Called Shakespeare Plays.* London, 1888. Reprint New York: AMS, 1972.

Dowling, Linda. *Hellenism and Homosexuality in Victorian Oxford.* Ithaca, N.Y.: Cornell University Press, 1994.

Economou, George. *The Goddess Natura in Medieval Literature.* Cambridge, Mass.: Harvard University Press, 1972.

Edelman, Lee. *Homographesis: Essays in Gay Literary and Cultural Theory.* New York: Routledge, 1994.

Eissler, K. R. *Leonardo da Vinci: Psychoanalytic Notes on the Enigma.* London: Hogarth Press, 1962.

Ellman, Richard. *Oscar Wilde.* New York: Vintage, 1988.

Fineman, Joel. *Shakespeare's Perjured Eye: The Invention of Poetic Subjectivity in the Sonnets.* Berkeley: University of California Press, 1986.

Flamel, Nicholas. *His Exposition of the Hieroglyphicall figures ... Together with The secret Booke of ARTEPHIUS.* London, 1624. Ed. Laurinda Dixon. New York: Garland, 1994.

Foucault, Michel. *Madness and Civilization: A History of Insanity in the Age of Reason.* Trans. Richard Howard. New York: Vintage, 1988.

————. "My Body, This Paper, This Fire." Trans. Geoff Bennington. *Oxford Literary Review* 4 (1979): 9–28.

————. *The Order of Things: An Archaeology of the Human Sciences.* New York: Random House, 1973.

Freud, Sigmund. *Gesammelte Werke, chronologische geordnet.* Ed. Anna Freud. 17 vols. London: Imago, 1940–52.

————. *The Standard Edition of the Complete Psychological Works of Sigmund Freud.* Trans. and ed. James Strachey et al. 24 vols. London: Hogarth Press, 1953–74.

Freud, Sigmund and Sándor Ferenczi. *The Correspondence of Sigmund Freud and Sándor Ferenczi.* Ed. Eva Brabant et al. 2 vols. Cambridge, Mass.: Belknap Press of Harvard University Press, 1993–96.

Freud, Sigmund and Wilhelm Fliess. *The Complete Letters of Sigmund Freud to Wilhelm Fliess, 1887–1904.* Trans. and ed. Jeffrey Moussaieff Masson. Cambridge, Mass.: Belknap Press of Harvard University Press, 1985.

Freud, Sigmund and Ernest Jones. *The Complete Correspondence of Sigmund Freud and Ernest Jones, 1908–1939.* Ed. R. Andrew Paskauskas. Cambridge, Mass.: Belknap Press of Harvard University Press, 1993.

Frye, Northrop. *Fearful Symmetry: A Study of William Blake.* Princeton, N.J.: Princeton University Press, 1947.

Fynsk, Christopher. "Between Ethics and Creation." *L'Esprit Créateur* 35, 3 (1995): 80–87.

Garnwell, Lynn and Richard Wells, eds. *Sigmund Freud and Art: His Personal Collection of Antiquities.* New York: Harry Abrams, 1989.

Goldberg, Jonathan. "*Romeo and Juliet*'s Open Rs." In *Queering the Renaissance*, ed. Jonathan Goldberg, 218–35. Durham, N.C.: Duke University Press, 1994.

Le Grand Robert de la langue française. 2nd ed. 9 vols. Paris: Le Robert, 1985.

Guillory, John. *Cultural Capital: The Problem of Literary Canon Formation.* Chicago: University of Chicago Press, 1993.

Harries, Martin. "Forgetting Lot's Wife: Artaud, Spectatorship, and Catastrophe." *Yale Journal of Criticism* 11,1 (1998): 221–38.

Harrap's Slang Dictionary/Dictionnaire. Ed. Georgette A Marks and Charles B. Johnson. Edinburgh: Harrap, 1993.

Hegel, Georg Wilhelm Friedrich. *Aesthetics: Lectures on Fine Art.* Trans. T. M. Knox. 2 vols. Oxford: Clarendon Press, 1975.

————. *Ästhetik.* 2 vols. Frankfurt am Main: Europäische Verlagsanstalt, 1966.

Heidegger, Martin. *Essais et conférences.* Trans. André Préau. Paris: Gallimard, 1958.

_____. *Poetry, Language, Thought*. Trans. Albert Hofstadter. New York: Harper and Row, 1971.

_____. *Vorträge und Aufsätze*. Pfullingen: Neskein, 1954.

Huber, Gérard. *L'Egypte ancienne dans la psychanalyse*. Paris: Masionneuve et Larose, 1987.

Hyde, H. Montgomery. *The Trials of Oscar Wilde*. New York: Dover, 1962.

Jones, Ernest. *The Life and Work of Sigmund Freud*. 3 vols. New York: Basic Books, 1953–57.

Jordan, Mark. *The Invention of Sodomy in Christian Theology*. Chicago: University of Chicago Press, 1997.

Knight, G. Wilson. *The Mutual Flame: On Shakespeare's Sonnets and The Phoenix and the Turtle*. London: Methuen, 1955.

Koestenbaum, Wayne. *Double Talk: The Erotics of Male Literary Collaboration*. New York: Routledge, 1989.

Kofman, Sarah. *The Childhood of Art: An Interpretation of Freud's Aesthetics*. Trans. Winifred Woodhull. New York: Columbia University Press, 1988.

Kopelson, Kevin. "Wilde, Barthes, and the Orgasmics of Truth." *Genders* 7 (1990): 22–31.

Lacan, Jacques. *The Ethics of Psychoanalysis, 1959–1960*. Trans. Dennis Porter. New York: W.W. Norton, 1992.

_____. *Le Séminaire de Jacques Lacan*. Vol. 7, *L'Ethique de la psychanalyse, 1959–1960*. Ed. Jacques-Alain Miller. Paris: Éditions du Seuil, 1986.

Laplanche, Jean. *Problématiques III: La Sublimation*. Paris: Presses Universitaires de France, 1980.

Lupton, Julia Reinhard and Kenneth Reinhard. *After Oedipus: Shakespeare in Psychoanalysis*. Ithaca, N.Y.: Cornell University Press, 1993.

Maclagan, Eric. "Leonardo in the Consulting Room." *Burlington Magazine* 42 (January 1923): 51–54.

Masson, Jeffrey Moussaieff. *The Assault on Truth: Freud's Suppression of the Seduction Theory*. New York: Farrar, Straus and Giroux, 1984.

Masten, Jeffrey. *Textual Intercourse: Collaboration, Authorship, and Sexualities in Renaissance Drama*. New York: Cambridge, 1997.

Mitchell, W. T. J. *Blake's Composite Art: A Study of the Illuminated Poetry*. Princeton, N.J.: Princeton University Press, 1978.

Muller, John P. and William J. Richardson, eds. *The Purloined Poe: Lacan, Derrida, and Psychoanalytic Reading*. Baltimore: Johns Hopkins University Press, 1988.

Pedretti, Carlo. "The Angel in the Flesh." *Achademia Leonardi Vinci: Journal of Leonardo Studies* 4 (1991): 34–51.

Pequigney, Joseph. *Such Is My Love: A Study of Shakespeare's Sonnets*. Chicago: University of Chicago Press, 1985.

Pfister, Oskar. "Kryptolalie, Kryptographie und unbewusstes Vexierbild bei Normalen." *Jahrbuch für Psychoanalytische und Psychopathologische Forschungen* 5 (1913): 117–56.

Richter, Simon. *Laocoon's Body and the Aesthetics of Pain*. Detroit: Wayne State University Press, 1992.

Rachjman, John. "Lacan and the Ethics of Modernity." *Representations* 15 (Summer 1986): 42–56.

Reinhard, Kenneth. "Freud, My Neighbor." *American Imago* 54, 2 (Summer 1997): 165–95.

———. "Kant with Sade, Lacan with Levinas." *MLN* 110, 4 (Sept. 1995): 785–808.

Ridge, Martin. *Ignatius Donnelly: The Portrait of a Politician.* Chicago: University of Chicago Press, 1962.

Rosenfeld, Eva M. "Dream and Vision: Some Remarks on Freud's Egyptian Bird Dream." *International Journal of Psychoanalysis* 37 (1956): 97–105.

Sade, Marquis de. *The 120 Days of Sodom and Other Writings.* Trans. Austryn Wainhouse and Richard Weaver. New York: Grove Pres, 1966.

Schapiro, Meyer. "Leonardo and Freud: An Art-Historical Study." *Journal of the History of Ideas* 17, 2 (1956): 147–78.

Schiesari, Juliana. "Mothers of Invention: Rereading Freud and Leonardo." In *Repossessions: Psychoanalysis and the Phantasms of Early Modern Culture,* ed. Timothy Murray and Alan K. Smith, 200–220. Minneapolis: University of Minnesota Press, 1998.

Shakespeare, William. *Shakespeare's Sonnets.* Ed. Stephen Booth. New Haven, Conn.: Yale University Press, 1977.

Showalter, Elaine. *Sexual Anarchy: Gender and Culture at the Fin de Siècle.* New York: Viking, 1990.

Vendler, Helen. *The Art of Shakespeare's Sonnets.* Cambridge, Mass.: Harvard University Press, 1997.

Vickers, Nancy "'The blazon of sweet beauty's best': Shakespeare's *Lucrece.*" In *Shakespeare and the Question of Theory,* ed. Patricia Parker and Geoffrey Hartman, 95–115. New York: Methuen, 1985.

———. "Diana Described: Scattered Women and Scattered Rhyme," In *Writing and Sexual Difference,* ed. Elizabeth Abel, 99–109. New York: Routledge, 1982.

Waddington, Raymond B. ""The Poetics of Eroticism: Shakespeare's 'Master-Mistress.'" In *Renaissance Discourses of Desire,* ed. Claude J. Summers and Ted-Larry Pebworth, 13–28. Columbia: University of Missouri Press, 1993.

Wilde, Oscar. *The Artist as Critic: Critical Writings of Oscar Wilde.* Ed. Richard Ellman. Chicago: University of Chicago Press, 1968.

Winckelmann, Johan Joachim. *Johann Joachim Winckelmanns Geschichte der Kunst des Altertums.* Heidelberg, 1882.

Wohl, Richard and Harry Trosman. "A Retrospect of Freud's *Leonardo.*" *Psychiatry* 18 (February 1955): 27–39.

Yerushalmi, Yosef Hayim. *Freud's Moses: Judaism Terminable and Interminable.* New Haven, Conn.: Yale University Press, 1991.

Žižek, Slavoj. *The Metastases of Enjoyment: Six Essays on Woman and Causality.* New York: Verso, 1994.

———. *The Sublime Object of Ideology.* New York: Verso, 1989.

Index

Acknowledgments

This is what Chaucer would call a "litel boke," and the list of people I bothered while composing it is correspondingly brief. But my gratitude is no less heartfelt for that. I wish to thank Joel Altman, Rhonda Garelick, Julia Lupton, Jeffrey Masten, Jeffrey Nunokawa, and Connie You for reading and commenting on drafts of chapters. Mark Jordan and Deborah Shuger replied promptly and helpfully to emailed queries. Jerome Singerman at the University of Pennsylvania Press shepherded the book into production with efficiency and good humor. Finally, I taught the subject of this book as a graduate course at Berkeley in the fall of 1998. The four students in that course—Erika Clowes, Drew Daniel, Joe Ring, and Snehal Shingavi—sharpened my arguments through their shrewd observations and patient questioning.

Earlier versions of several pages of Chapter 4 originally appeared in "Creation: Lacan in Kansas," in an electronic journal, *Journal for Culture and Religious Theory* 2, 1 (December 2000). I thank the editors for permission to reprint this material here.